FIFTY YEARS AT THE PIT

50 years at THE PIT

The University of New Mexico's Legendary Venue

GARY HERRON
FOREWORD BY HUNTER GREENE

UNIVERSITY OF NEW MEXICO PRESS | ALBUQUERQUE

Library of Congress Cataloging-in-Publication Data
Names: Herron, Gary (Sports editor), author.
Title: Fifty years at the Pit: The University of New Mexico's Legendary Venue / Gary Herron;
    foreword by Hunter Greene.
Description: Albuquerque: University of New Mexico Press, 2018. | Includes bibliographical
    references. |
Identifiers: LCCN 2017017757 (print) | LCCN 2017044287 (ebook) | ISBN 9780826359414 (E-book) |
    ISBN 9780826359407 (printed case: alk. paper)
Subjects: LCSH: New Mexico Lobos (Basketball team)—History. | University of New Mexico—
    Basketball—History.
Classification: LCC GV885.43.U539 (ebook) | LCC GV885.43.U539 H47 2018 (print) | DDC
    796.323/630978961—dc23 LC record available at https://lccn.loc.gov/2017017757

Cover photographs: Courtesy J. B. Gallegos, UNM Athletics, and Tim March for Moji Photography.
Designed by Lila Romero and Melissa Tandysh
Composed in Gotham and Vitesse

NCAA.com voted the Pit one of "The Top Five Loudest, Most-Intimidating Places to Play."

Sports Illustrated ranked the Pit among the top 20 sporting venues in the country.

USA Today ranked the Pit in its "Ten Great Places to Get Pumped for NCAA Action."

Fox Sports proclaimed the Pit one of the top 10 "old school" college basketball arenas in the country.

Contents

Foreword

I am honored that author Gary Herron asked me to write a foreword for his book about the Pit. I just wonder why it took so long for someone to come up with the great idea to commemorate such a unique venue full of energy, history, and excitement.

Coach Gary Colson and his staff were major factors in my choice to come to the University of New Mexico; they offered me a chance to improve my game and perform in the legendary Pit. Colson was a great coach, and we had great teams. I will always remember Gary for what he did for me. After growing up in Los Angeles as a huge Lakers fan, I found the Lobo experience similar to the atmosphere and fan adoration that the Lakers enjoyed. It was a fantastic experience that few get to appreciate. I am forever grateful that I was able to play in the Pit.

After I finished my college career and played a short stint overseas, I chose to return not to LA but to Albuquerque because it had become my home. I love Albuquerque—the people and the way of life. I chose to raise my family here.

In 2014 I had the opportunity to return to the Pit as the color commentator for Lobo basketball. It's great working alongside Robert Portnoy and being back in action, even if it's on the sidelines. I feel it's a way to give back to the fans by helping them appreciate the nuances of the game and offering insight from a former Lobo player's perspective.

Playing in the Pit was a fantastic experience that few get to appreciate, and I am forever grateful that I was able to play in in such a dynamic venue. I hope you enjoy *Fifty Years at the Pit*!

HUNTER GREENE, UNM BASKETBALL PLAYER,
1983–1988

The new and improved logo designed in 2010 for University Arena, a.k.a. the Pit and, for a few years, a.k.a. WisePies Arena. But "the Pit" is its best-known moniker. Courtesy UNM Athletics.

Acknowledgments

When the University of New Mexico Press asked me to help find someone to write this book, I tossed out several names—guys who were passionate about Lobos basketball, guys who had attended many games, and even guys who were better writers than me.

But soon it dawned on me: Why not me? Although I don't go to many UNM basketball games (as the sports editor at the *Rio Rancho Observer* I am consumed with high school sports), I have been to the Pit hundreds of times, seen some of the packed-Pit games with the University of Las Vegas (UNLV) and Arizona, covered countless high school basketball state-tournament games, attended every Ty Murray Invitational held there, seen concerts and graduations, and cracked up while watching the Harlem Globetrotters entertain on the floor. I've also seen a few boxing cards there, and I watched tennis great Bjorn Borg play on the Pit floor in 1983.

So I had my answer to "Why not me?"

After several months of hard work, I want to send out a big thank-you to everyone who helped put this book together. I especially want to thank those who provided photographs and other key information: Frank Mercogliano of UNM's sports information department (a.k.a. media relations), former UNM women's coach Don Flanagan, and local photographers J. B. Gallegos, Tim March, and Vincent Maisano.

This book is dedicated to the millions of people who entered the Pit to enjoy an event over the past five decades.

Chapter 1

The "King" of UNM Basketball

Who would have thought back in the sixties that a 37-foot-deep hole would eventually hold one of the most famous college basketball venues in the United States?

That venue, officially named the University Arena but known near and far as the Pit, is one of the most recognized venues in all of sports. In 1999 the Pit was recognized by *Sports Illustrated* as one of the top 20 sporting venues of the twentieth century.

It all started as a 37-foot-deep hole, thanks to the efforts of UNM men's basketball coach Bob King and his ability to turn a losing program into a respectable one that needed a larger venue.

The 2015–2016 season was the 50th year that WisePies Arena—fondly dubbed the Pit—served as the home for Lobo hoops. The Lobos averaged 13,031 fans per game over 16 home games in 2015–2016, playing basketball in front of a total of 208,492 fans inside the arena. The Lobos led the Mountain West Conference (MWC) in attendance, were 23rd in attendance in the nation, and were nearly 6,000 fans over the league's average attendance. To top it off, it was a season that ended short of a postseason tournament.

The first game in the Pit was played on December 1, 1966, a 62–53 UNM win over Abilene Christian.

In the 2016–2017 season, the Pit's 51st season, the Lobos were to play 17 games inside the arena, including 8 games out of MWC play. The nonconference home slate included current and old rivals New Mexico State and the University of Texas at El Paso (UTEP), as well a 50-year anniversary game against Abilene Christian—the Lobos' first opponent in the Pit. That game was played on November 30.

The Lobos returned 10 players from 2015 to 2016, including four starters. That returning class was highlighted by Elijah Brown and Tim Williams, the only two players returning to MWC action who had averaged 16 points or more in the last season. Both earned All-MWC first-team honors from the media, marking the first time the Lobos have returned multiple All-MWC first-team honorees.

Through their first 50 seasons, over 13 million fans flocked into the sunken edifice to see their beloved Lobos play basketball. The Lobos averaged an astounding 15,410 fans over that half century. The Lobos have finished second in the nation in attendance five times, third on four occasions, and fourth six times, and they have been in the top 25 in attendance in each of the first 50 years.

Until the Pit opened for business in December 1966, the Lobos had played in Johnson Gym, on the UNM campus just north of busy Central Avenue, back then known as Route 66. Before that, Carlisle Gym, also on the UNM campus, had been their home from 1928 until 1957, when Johnson Gym opened.

Born August 24, 1923, in Gravity, Iowa, Bob King came to New Mexico in 1962 after serving three seasons as an assistant coach at the University of Iowa. He understood that changing the landscape of Lobo basketball would not be an easy thing to do.

Back then, Albuquerque was more of a football town. In 1964 the football team had not suffered a losing season since 1958, while the basketball team had seen eight consecutive losing seasons (from 1954 through 1962). In Coach Bob Sweeney's final three seasons, UNM was 6–19 (1959–1960), 6–17 (1960–1961), and 6–20 (1961–1962).

Thus a new arena was probably the farthest thing from King's mind; there were no sellouts at Roy Johnson Gym (named after Roy Johnson, the UNM coach from 1919 to 1931), which the Lobos had opened with a 68–52 win over Western Michigan on December 6, 1957. But Johnson Gym could only seat 6,332 fans, which probably seemed sufficient when it opened because the team's previous facility, Carlisle Gym, had a limit of 2,010.

King believed that fundamentals were the key, and he wanted to recruit large, defensive players who would give it their all on the hardwood. He began by recruiting a Detroit native, Ira Harge, who King had seen play at Burlington Junior College in Iowa. It was a good move: in just two seasons (1962–1964) Harge became the first Lobo to score 1,000 points. Adding to his big-man roster with the likes of Claude Williams, Joe McKay, Mike Lucero, and Skip Kruzich, King's first season at the helm began with four consecutive wins—the first three at Johnson Gym—and ended with a record of 16–9.

In King's second season, the Lobos went 23–6 and won the Western Athletic Conference (WAC) with a 7–3 record, although they lost again in the National Invitation Tournament (NIT) final in the Big Apple, 86–54 to Bradley, after a 72–65 victory over New York University. It wasn't a mirage: King led UNM to a 19–8 mark in 1964–1965, which also ended with a loss in the NIT, this time in the first round, 61–54 to St. John's.

Another great season came in 1965–1966: 16–8, including a hard-fought, overtime loss, 67–64, to Texas Western—the team that legendary Don Haskins would lead to the National Collegiate Athletic Association (NCAA) championship after its victory over Adolph Rupp's all-white Kentucky Wildcats.

This photo was called the "1903 Champions," which is strange because, according to the UNM media guide, the 1903 team had a record of 1–2, with all three of its games against the "Albuquerque Minors." Courtesy UNM Athletics.

Lobo John Teel (number 52) seen in action during the 1957–1958 season, the first season the Lobos played at then-new Johnson Gym. Courtesy UNM Athletics.

Looking to the north, with the UNM softball complex (lower left) and Santa Ana Star Field and UNM's baseball diamond, (lower right). In the middle is the Pit. Across the street is the long-gone Albuquerque Sports Stadium, then the home of the Albuquerque Dukes. Courtesy UNM Athletics.

How the Pit looked before the $60 million renovation that began in 2009, as seen from its northeast corner. Courtesy UNM Athletics.

So, along with more wins and many more fans, it was time for a bigger gym.

University President Tom Popejoy hired Pete McDavid as the university's athletic director. McDavid opted to get architect Joe Boehning—Class of 1949 Albuquerque High grad, and a UNM graduate—on board. The university signed the construction contract in December of 1965 with K. L. House Construction Co. of Albuquerque. (Mr. Boehning passed away in December 2016.)

First, a unique Behlen roof measuring 338 feet by 300 feet was set up by contractors, and then the 37-foot hole was carved out, with an estimated 55,000 cubic yards of earth removed. About 28,000 yards of concrete were then poured into the initial construction, which allowed a seating capacity of 14,831, including chairbacks and bench-style seating, with the original chairbacks in orange, gold, and yellow. The floor had a 6-inch layer of concrete holding the subfloor supports. The distance from the ceiling to the floor measured 56 feet, and there was a 10-foot margin around the playing area. The floor was lit by 100 mercury-vapor lamps, each producing 110 candlepower.

Boehning said at the time that it was the only basketball arena in the United States where all of the seating was below ground level. To that point, there were 44 rows of seats, and if you thought you were lucky to get a ticket in row 1, you'd be dismayed when you arrived at the arena and found you were at the top of the arena, just off the concourse.

Try to guess the price of the building. You probably can't. It was an incredibly economical $1.5 million.

"We've built this arena for nearly $1.5 million," UNM President Tom Popejoy told *Albuquerque Tribune* columnist Carlos Salazar at the time. "There are structures comparable in size that cost between $4 million and $5 million. We have eliminated costly masonry work by the use of compacted dirt to support the seating areas—a money-saving idea we learned in the construction of our 30,000-seat football stadium."

Twin super scoreboards were yet to be installed two days before the opener, and, opined Salazar, "It would be embarrassing for the Lobos to play their opener using chalk and a blackboard to follow the action."

Salazar, a 1987 inductee of the New Mexico (back then the Albuquerque) Sports Hall of Fame, even took time in his November 29, 1966, column to explain something to fans:

There's a reason for the numbering of rows from the top down—a practice that differs from traditional systems. The top row is No. 1 and the bottom is row 32 in the theatre-style section and 43 in the bench-style sections.

Aside from the fact that all seats are reached from the top down, there is the problem of numbering seats in rows that are 'created' in the corner areas as the encircling tiers get larger.

Regardless of where they sat, or if they even understood why their row 1 seat was just below the concourse, fans apparently loved their Lobos—and soon their new facility. In 1966–1967 the team went 19–8, winning 14 of its 15 games in its new home and averaging 15,724 fans per game—second in the nation.

Expansion was undertaken when it became apparent that fan interest was too great even for the original structure. The 1975 expansion (King was gone by then, coaching at Indiana State for three seasons from 1975 to 1978) cost about $1.8 million and involved the extension of a cantilevered deck above the existing facility. There are six rows in that deck, with a seating capacity of 2,300. Reserved standing-room-only spots increased the Pit's capacity to 18,018.

Various shots of University Arena during its construction period; you can see how the roof was assembled before the floor area was totally built out. Courtesy UNM Athletics.

Before the 1990–1991 season there was another renovation, this time a $1.1 million facelift. The interior was totally repainted, the restrooms were remodeled, a new public-address system was installed, concession stands and the ticket office were upgraded, and TV monitors were installed at concession stands so fans wouldn't miss any action. In addition, more handicapped seating was added.

On October 2, 1992, UNM President Richard Peck announced that the basketball court in the building would be named in honor of King:

> We wanted to recognize Coach King's contributions to Lobo basketball. UNM's Memorial Committee recommended that we honor Coach King's accomplishments, and the naming of the court has allowed us to do so without diminishing the recognition, which has already been paid to his colleagues, including former Director of Athletics Pete McDavid.
>
> Bob King Court and the Pete McDavid Lounge are a tribute to two of the men who are responsible for the success of the facility we fondly call the Pit.

Bob King Court was dedicated at formal ceremonies on November 28, 1992, and Coach King was there, enjoying every minute of it, as the Lobos played an exhibition game against the Lithuanian national team that evening.

Although he'd last coached two decades earlier, Bob King's legacy wasn't ever to be forgotten. This architect of Lobo basketball was also responsible for the creation of the Lobo Invitational, UNM's post-Christmas tournament and the fifth-oldest regular season tournament in the nation. New Mexico's annual Most Valuable Player (MVP) award is also named in his honor: the Bob King MVP Award for men's basketball. King was inducted into the Albuquerque Sports Hall of Fame in 1982, the University

Top Left: Pete McDavid was the athletics director at UNM when the Pit was being built. McDavid graduated from UNM in 1938 and went into coaching, first at Santa Fe High School and then at Albuquerque High School. He became the athletic director at UNM in 1956. Courtesy UNM Athletics.

Top right: Three different photos of University Arena as it was being built, circa 1966. Courtesy UNM Athletics.

Bottom right: The sports page of the November 29, 1966, Albuquerque Tribune, with a column about the new basketball arena by the late Carlos Salazar, a member of the New Mexico Sports Hall of Fame.

BEHLEN DUBL-PANL ROOF

of New Mexico Athletic Hall of Fame in 1987, and the Indiana State University Athletics Hall of Fame in 1999.

Coach King passed away December 10, 2004, in the Veteran's Administration Hospital in Albuquerque at the age of 81. The University observed a moment of silence before that night's women's basketball game against Bowling Green and again several days later before the men's game against Arkansas-Pine Bluff. Services for Coach King were held December 15 in the Pit. A viewing was held for 90 minutes before the public service. The burial took place later at the National Cemetery in Santa Fe.

"The State of New Mexico as well as the nation has lost one of the finest basketball minds to ever coach the game," said New Mexico State head coach Lou Henson. "Bob King was the guiding force that brought the UNM basketball program into national prominence. His contributions to the State of New Mexico are immeasurable."

"I always felt to follow in the shadow and footsteps of Bob [King] and Norm [Ellenberger] was a privilege for me coming from a smaller school like

Top: The view from the bottom of the "famous" ramp, where opponents get their first view of the Pit filled up with adoring Lobos fans. Courtesy UNM Athletics.

Bottom: Here's another view from the bottom of the ramp, looking back up, where teams gather before running down to the Pit floor. Courtesy UNM Athletics.

The view of the ramp that leads to the Pit floor, with the "intimidating" reference to the altitude: "A mile high and louder than ——" (something that rhymes with "Pit"). Courtesy UNM Athletics.

Pepperdine," said Gary Colson, UNM's head coach for eight seasons from 1980 to 1988. "It was a real streak of luck that I got to the University of New Mexico."

"We're very mindful of coach King's legacy. I'm one of the proud benefactors of the values and principles he instilled, and the impact he made on his players and peers," said then–head coach Ritchie McKay. McKay's father, Joe, played for King as a senior in 1962–1963.

"More than 40 years ago, Bob King had a vision for the University of New Mexico," said UNM Director of Athletics Rudy Davalos. "And, it's a vision that all Lobo fans have to this day. The success the basketball programs have enjoyed—both men's and women's—is a direct result of the foundation he laid for future coaches and players. I really enjoyed my association with Bob and his family over the past 12 years. He was a classy gentleman who will be missed by many people, but never forgotten."

King was gone, but the Pit lived on.

UNM announced in December 2014 that Wise-Pies Pizza & Salad, a locally owned business, had agreed to give a $5 million cash gift over 10 years to support the UNM Athletics Department through the newly established WisePies Fund. It was the largest cash gift ever to UNM Athletics and the sixth-largest cash gift overall to the university. The WisePies

I'll never forget being at the microphone, when the Pit opened, on December 1, 1966, nor the game many remember, in which Royce Olney beat Utah.

—Mike Roberts
(voice of the Lobos, 1966–2008);
February 1, 1998;
UNM 77, Utah 74

An aerial view of the Pit floor, shot from the top of the southeast corner. This is from "back in the day," before it became Bob King Court, and long before the $60 million renovation project. Courtesy UNM Athletics.

Fund was to be used to support the Pit debt service incurred during the 2009–2010 renovations.

In recognition of WisePies's generous support, the University Arena was renamed the WisePies Arena for the duration of the gift, though it is still fondly called the Pit. The company logo appeared on exterior signage of the arena as well as on the Bob King Court and on tickets. The recognition also included an arena suite.

"From the time we first discussed the potential renovation of the Pit, we talked about the need for state and private support to make the renovation a reality," Paul Krebs said. "Specifically, we've talked about the need to find a naming rights partner for the building. The fact that WisePies is a local company and Steve Chavez, the company's co-CEO, is a native New Mexican and successful, local

businessman, makes this gift even more significant and special."

"We look forward to partnering with Wise-Pies on future endeavors," said Tim Cline, senior vice president for Learfield Sports, UNM Athletics' multimedia-rights holder. "Our Lobo Sports Properties staff aligns with Paul and his team on a daily basis, and we're proud to have such a great partner in the University of New Mexico." The legacy of King continues, even today. At every game in the Pit, you can find people fondly remembering King as the Lobos' coach.

Take a walk around the concourse and see Lobo highlights, by decade, throughout the arena. There were highlights, of course, before the Pit opened a half century ago. But the Pit is where the memories linger . . .

A Look at "The Architect's" First Season in the Pit

Opening its doors for business on December 1, 1966, the sixth-ranked Lobos beat Abilene Christian 62–53.

The game initiated the first of what would be six seasons for coach Bob King and the Lobos in the Pit. An appreciative, interested crowd of 12,020 turned out. The *Albuquerque Tribune* reported the next day—on its front page, no less—that the building emptied in four and a half minutes.

Prior to the 1966 opener, the *Tribune* remarked, "To the 'core' of the team—Mel Daniels, Ben Monroe, Don Hoover, Bill Morgan, Ron Nelson, Ron Sanford, Howie Grimes, and Steve Shropshire—we say, 'Go get them, Lobos.'"

It was a magical place, not only for the team and its success in its new building, but also for the growing legion of fans. It's a place where fans stand and clap at the start of each half, only seating themselves after both teams have scored.

And, as countless players have seen on their way down the ramp to the floor, it's a quick welcome to the Pit, "A mile high and louder than ——!" Everyone knows what that missing word is, even though it's not loud at all.

In their first season playing in the Pit, the Lobos went 19–8, and despite an unimpressive 5–5 mark

The 1966–1967 UNM media guide, which cost only a dollar. Courtesy UNM Athletics.

Len Lopez was a Lobo for the Pit's first three seasons, playing in just eight games in 1966–1967, then 26 games the next season and 23 as a senior. Courtesy UNM Athletics.

in WAC games, they earned a trip to the NIT in New York City. There, the Lobos beat Syracuse 66–64, and then fell to Rutgers 65–60.

An interesting note from that first season in the Pit: The games played there were part of an experiment to tinker with the free-throw rules. Except for the games involving North Dakota and Seattle, which didn't agree to the pilot program, no free throws were to be awarded until a team was assessed its seventh foul in each half. (Fouls committed during the act of shooting still put the offended player at the foul line.)

"The purpose of the experiment is to determine the effect and desirability of further curtailment of free-throwing," said WAC Commissioner Paul Brechler.

Check out the team's record in the Pit in the building's early going: 14–1 in 1966–1967; 16–2 in 1967–1968; 12–2 in 1968–1969; 10–4 in 1969–1970; 10–5 in 1970–1971; and 12–2 in 1971–1972. The Lobos had double-digit home-court wins every year and attendance ranging from an average of 11,920 (1967–1968) to 14,144 (1970–1971) fans each season, ranking anywhere from second to sixth nationally.

The 1967–1968 team won its first 17 games, spending what remained of the 1968 portion of its schedule in the national top 10. By the end of the season, the Lobos were WAC champions, going 8–2 in the conference, with both WAC losses taking place away from the Pit.

This team also gave the Pit one of its top victories and best-ever games when fifth-ranked Utah came to Albuquerque to play sixth-ranked New Mexico. The Lobos' talented quintet all scored in double figures, and the Lobos won 72–66. The

Top Left: Coach Bob King and Howard Grimes, who came to UNM from New Lennox, Illinois. Courtesy UNM Athletics.

Top right: Terry Schaafsma came off the bench for coach Bob King in 1967–1968 and 1968–1969. Courtesy UNM Athletics.

Bottom right: Keith Griffith played in 22 games in each the second and third (1967–1968 and 1968–1969) seasons of the Pit; later, he was a color commentator for radio play-by-play man Mike Roberts. Courtesy UNM Athletics.

Dave Culver played for UNM the second, third, and fourth seasons the Pit was in use. Here, he poses for a preseason photo with coach Bob King. Courtesy UNM Athletics.

victory earned UNM its first invitation to the NCAA Tournament, finally surpassing the NIT as the tournament to be in during those days. King was named the WAC's Coach of the Year.

Norm Ellenberger arrived in time for the 1967–1968 season, becoming coach King's top assistant. A 1955 graduate of Butler University, Ellenberger had been the head basketball and baseball coach at Monmouth after an outstanding prep career in the Hoosier State, before coming to UNM. (Lobos baseball coach Bob Leigh was also an assistant, having joined King in 1966–1967.)

That 1967–1968 Lobo squad was what many fans considered his best team. It included All-American Ron Nelson and Academic All-American Ron Becker on the wings, and Ron Sanford and Greg "Stretch" Howard in the paint, the latter an intimidating presence inside. And Howard Grimes

Mickey Sego came up with this caricature of Bob King as the Lobos were preparing for the 1968–1969 season, the third for the Pit. Courtesy UNM Athletics.

provided the perfect complement as the power forward: part brawler, part garbage man—and an enforcer defensively.

That team went 23–5 and won the WAC, winning 8 of its 10 WAC contests.

Those seasons of 1966–1967 and 1967–1968 might have pushed the frenzy for Lobo basketball to a new high. That success also helped bring out the ugly side of the "fish bowl." With Lobo basketball, sometimes it's a question of "What have you done lately?"

In 1968–1969 the Lobos added Willie Long and Petie Gibson to their returning foundation of Howard, Sanford, Becker, and Grimes. It was a talented team expected to challenge for another WAC title and push its way into the national rankings, but surprisingly they finished 4–6—last in the WAC.

The 1968 Lobo Invitational All-Tournament team was made up of (left to right) Pete Cross (San Francisco), Charles Yelverton (Fordham), Petie Gibson (UNM), John Baum (Temple), and Willie Long (UNM). Courtesy UNM Athletics.

Tommy Roberts played for the Lobos from 1970–1973, averaging 9.8 points per game as a starting guard in his junior season and 7.1 points per game as a senior. Courtesy UNM Athletics.

I'll never forget when we played the UTEP Miners (67–55) in 1974 by beating the Bear, Don Haskins; we won the WAC championship. I was a junior, coming off the bench—it was a great experience. We had a big celebration in the locker room; Haskins came in there and congratulated us.

—Bob Toppert (1972–1975)
(Toppert was one of King's last recruits and a member of the first UNM team to win an NCAA game.)

Petie Gibson (number 10) played for the Lobos from 1968–1971. He still lives and works in Albuquerque and is still regarded as one of the all-time favorites. Courtesy UNM Athletics.

Caricature covers were featured in the 1967–1968 season; this one is from the Lobos' 82–67 victory over Creighton on December 22, 1967. Courtesy Gary Herron.

Caricature covers were still around in the 1970–1971 season; this one is from UNM's 72–45 rout of Northern Colorado on December 12, 1970. Courtesy Gary Herron.

In 1969–1970 the Lobos went 13–13 and 7–7 in league play. In 1970–1971, UNM finished two games above .500 at 14–12 but staggered to a 4–10 finish in the WAC—seventh out of eight teams. In 1971–1972 the Lobos went 15–11 overall but posted their fourth consecutive non-winning season in the WAC. It also was King's and the Lobos' fourth season without an invitation to postseason play.

The waters in what became regarded as a "fish bowl" were swirling—and King was not immune to those swirling waters.

But, in addition to the downward trend in success on the hardwood, there was another reason some were calling for a change: King had that promising, young assistant (Norm Ellenberger) storming the sidelines and seducing the Pit with his energy and personality. He had the looks of a Las Vegas nightclub singer, wore turquoise around his neck, and promised to add run-and-gun to hard-nosed defense.

So King was out and Ellenberger was in after the turbulent 1971–1972 season.

Still, King had set the bar pretty high for those who would follow: He compiled an overall mark of 175–89 and never had a losing record in 10 seasons. Before King's arrival, the Lobos had endured eight straight losing seasons. He remains the coach with the second most winnings in UNM history. His Lobo program produced 10 All-WAC performers and 3 All-Americans (Mel Daniels, Ron Nelson, and Willie Long).

After King left UNM, he served as the Indiana State University head basketball coach from 1975 to 1978—along the way elevating the Sycamores' program to Division I status, where he produced an overall record of 61–24. His .718 winning percentage ranks third all-time in school history, trailing only John Wooden (.746) and Glenn M. Curtis (.724), while his 61 victories rank eighth in Sycamore men's basketball history.

In his three seasons as the head coach at Indiana State, King steered the Sycamores to NIT berths in 1977 and 1978, while assembling components for the acclaimed 1978–1979 NCAA men's basketball runner-up team.

King also served as the director of athletics at Indiana State from 1974 to 1980. In seven eventful years, he transformed Indiana State's image as a small college athletics power, rich in tradition, into a formidable national force.

King suffered a stroke before the start of the 1978–1979 basketball season and was forced to step down as the head basketball coach. Bill Hodges was named the interim coach, and he led the Sycamores to the NCAA Championship game—a contest many college basketball fans recall as it pitted Michigan State, led by Earvin "Magic" Johnson, against the Indiana State Sycamores, led by that tow-headed kid from French Lick, Indiana, Larry Bird. (They would have countless meetings in the NBA in the seasons that followed.)

King would not return to coaching on account of health reasons. In his later years, he and his wife, Sharel, lived in a comfortable home in Los Chavez, south of Albuquerque, and enjoyed venturing to nearby Belen High School, where their sons, Brad and Randy, played for the Eagles.

Willie Long goes in for a layup in the Lobos' 76–47 blowout of Brown on January 4, 1969. Courtesy UNM Athletics.

- **December 1, 1966:** The Pit's inaugural game. Mel Daniels turns in a double-double with 19 points and 12 rebounds. UNM holds Abilene Christian to just 40 shots from the field while launching 57 of its own, and out-rebounds its foe 37-16.

- **February 23, 1967:** Ben Monroe sets a lofty benchmark for years to come, scoring 41 points (remember, there were no 3-point shots then) in a 97-75 victory over visiting Brigham Young University (BYU). The record lasted more than nine years, until Iowa's Bruce King notched 42 points in a Lobo Invitational game vs. Pitt. The first Lobo to top Monroe's mark was Marvin Johnson, with 46 points, in December 1977.

- **January 18, 1968:** It's fifth-ranked Utah versus the sixth-ranked Lobos, and five Lobos get into the double-figure scoring column, led by Ron Nelson's 15, to edge the Utah Utes 72–66. Unranked 30 days later, the Utes got their revenge in Salt Lake City, 71–64, dropping the Lobos from fifth to seventh in the rankings.

- **February 7, 1968:** Ron Sanford scores a game-high 23 points, while NMSU's Jimmy Collins pours in 21 and 6th-ranked UNM beats the 10th-ranked Aggies 72-71 as Greg "Stretch" Howard cans a free throw with seven seconds left in the game. The lead changed hands 14 times before Howard's final free throw.

- **March 16, 1968:** Because of NCAA rules, "Stretch" Howard, as a transfer, isn't allowed to play in this NCAA Tournament game, one night after Santa Clara downed UNM 86-73. The Aggies—swept in the regular season—hold on for a 62-58 victory. Ron Nelson scores 26 and the "other" Ron, Sanford, notches 23, but the rest of the Lobos combine for only 9 points. The night before, Pit fans had an opportunity to see Lew Alcindor and the University of California, Los Angeles (UCLA), on their way to another national championship, beat the Aggies 58–49.

- **February 1, 1969:** A 20-point win over the Aggies in Las Cruces earlier in the season didn't mean anything: the Lobos had a 4-point lead with 10 seconds to go, only to see the Aggies tie them at 66. King called a timeout with 5 seconds to play and Petie Gibson wound up with the ball at midcourt—after a Ron Nelson miss—and jacked up a buzzer-beating 25-footer for a thrilling 68–66 victory.

- **February 12, 1972:** Mike Faulkner leads the Lobos with 25 points and a dozen rebounds in a 77–75 win in overtime over Colorado State.

- **March 3, 1972:** Darryl Minniefield pulls down a Pit record 23 rebounds in the Lobos' 77-58 victory over Utah. It's coach Bob King's final victory at UNM; the next night, seventh-ranked BYU beats the Lobos 61-60 in his finale at the helm.

Stormin' Norman (1972–1979) and Beyond

After legendary Bob King (1963–1972) left UNM, coaches came and went with varying degrees of success: some won conference titles, some got the Lobos to the NIT, and others managed to get the Lobos to the NCAA Tournament, but with limited success. As the twenty-first century approached, many UNM Lobo basketball coaches came and went; they, along with some of their most memorable games, are included here.

Norm Ellenberger (1972–1979; 134–62)

"Lobogate" is the word that often comes to mind when Ellenberger's name comes up—but not before some great, memorable years, and the introduction of the slogan, "Make It Happen." Surprisingly, basketball may not have been his best sport: he played several seasons in the Pittsburgh Pirates' organization after graduating from Butler in 1955.

"I guarantee fans we'll put on a show," Ellenberger said before taking the reins from King for the 1972–1973 season. He was right: King had produced two 20-game win seasons in his 10 years in Johnson Gym and the Pit. Ellenberger, rolling off

Top right: Mark Saiers (number 21), who played for the Lobos from 1971–1974, is seen here in a 1972 game. Saiers was a team captain. Courtesy UNM Athletics.

Top left: Darryl Minniefield played his junior season (1971–1972) for coach Bob King, and then his senior season, averaging 13.1 points per game, for new coach Norm Ellenberger. He was a fourth-round draft pick of the Philadelphia 76ers in 1973. Courtesy UNM Athletics.

Bottom left: Ricky Williams saw 300 minutes of action as a freshman in 1974–1975, with coach Norm Ellenberger noting he sent him in to "make things happen." He once scored 24 points in a single quarter as a prep player in New York. Courtesy UNM Athletics.

Left: Norm Cacy, seen here at the foul line, played for UNM from 1974 to 1976. He came to UNM from Manzano High School, playing in what was then a freshman-record 412 minutes in 25 games in 1974–1975. Courtesy UNM Athletics.

Right: Steve Davis, who came to UNM from Clovis, made the program cover for the Lobos' December 9, 1975, game against New Mexico State. Courtesy Gary Herron.

King's foundation, threw out 20-game win seasons in his first two seasons in the Pit.

In 1972–1973 the Lobos went 21–6 overall and 9–5 in conference games, finishing only behind WAC champ Arizona State. UNM won 12 of 15 games down the stretch, returning to the national rankings for the first time in three seasons, and that paid off in a trip to New York City. There, in famed Madison Square Garden, they lost in the NIT 65–63 to Virginia Tech. That meant UNM had lost its last three games of the season.

The next season opened with 12 straight wins and a number 8 ranking, which disappeared after consecutive road losses at Arizona, Arizona State, and UTEP. UNM racked up a 10–4 WAC record, averaging 84.2 points a game, with an average winning margin of 12.3 points. By the season's end, UNM had scored 100 or more points six times.

Ellenberger and his staff managed to right the ship, as the Lobos won 10 of their final 14 games, which included the WAC championship game, a 67–65 win over visiting UTEP, giving them three WAC titles and a 73–65 victory over Idaho State at a 1974 NCAA West Regional in Pocatello, Idaho, which sent UNM to a West Regional showdown in Tucson.

The NCAA run was a short one: ranked 17th, UNM lost to San Francisco 64–61 in Tucson, then won a meaningless NCAA consolation game there, 66–61 over 20th-ranked Dayton, which had taken UCLA into triple overtime in falling the night before.

The 22-7 overall mark and 10–4 run through the WAC gave Ellenberger credence, but he wanted to make his future teams more special—he opted to feed off the Pit's frenetic fans and have his teams press and run-and-gun, tiring foes along the way with that style combined with Albuquerque's altitude. But that would take a little while; UNM was a lackluster 13–13 (4–10 in the WAC) in 1974–1975.

But Ellenberger liked what he saw in Las Vegas, where a coach named Jerry "The Shark" Tarkanian had electrified a city with his UNLV 'Runnin' Rebels. Ellenberger was coming off that hiccup season in 1974–1975. He wanted to change the face of Lobo basketball. So he did.

The athleticism of the Lobos took a jump up. Ellenberger went the junior college route for some quick fixes, and those tactics earned New Mexico

Norm Ellenberger is seen twice on the cover of the Lobos' 1975–1976 media guide, with assistant coach John Whisenant (lower left) sharing a photo with him. "Whiz" coached the International Basketball League's short-lived New Mexico Slam from 1999–2001. Courtesy UNM Athletics.

the nickname "Transfer Tech." The program was ripe with two-year players. The Lobo fans didn't mind much. They came to see exciting, winning basketball. They got it.

At the expense of being touted nationally as "Transfer U," a bunch of JuCo transfers started paving the way for more excitement.

The Lobos of 1975–1976 played at a quicker pace behind a starting lineup of Larry Gray, George Berry, Rick Williams, Dale Slaughter, and Mike Patterson. They ran to a 16–11 overall mark and went 8–6 in the WAC.

A ticket stub from one of the Lobos' most memorable games of all time in the Pit, albeit an 80–73 loss to fourth-ranked UNLV on January 17, 1976, in front of a full house. Courtesy Gary Herron.

Top: Coach Norm Ellenberger and some of his Lobos, including popular Gabe Nava (number 14), killed September 10, 1981, at Ned's El Portal in a robbery. Courtesy UNM Athletics.

Bottom: Coach Norm Ellenberger (left end of the bench) and his players look like they're sensing a loss in the Pit. The local media are seen in the row right behind them. Courtesy UNM Athletics.

Top: "Make It Happen" was the slogan imprinted on T-shirts and this souvenir postseason program from the very successful 1977–1978 season, highlighted with the WAC championship, which was followed by a disappointing loss to Cal State–Fullerton in an NCAA Tournament first-round game. Courtesy Gary Herron.

Bottom: A program from the 1978 NCAA Western Region Championships, played in the Pit March 16 and 18, 1978, where UNM would have been if not for the loss to Cal State–Fullerton. The program set fans back two bucks. Courtesy Gary Herron.

"

I'll never forget when Marvin Johnson lived up to his 'Automatic' nickname and scorched Colorado State for 50 points. Fifty—still the UNM and WAC record. Automatic was just that–21-of-27 shooting—with his smooth jumper, 8-of-10 free throws on a chilly March evening in 1978. Not many remember that he busted his school record, which was 46. . . . The next day, I got to hang out with Marvin at the UNM Student Union Building, basking in his aura and writing a story that ran in the *Journal* the next day. Hundreds of students came by to acknowledge Marvin, shake his hand, touch his shoulder, hug him, and tell how special he was.

—Bart Ripp (*Albuquerque Journal* beat writer, 1975–1979)

One of the most popular Lobos from the "Make It Happen" days was Michael Cooper, who lasted longer in the Duke City than this Southwest Sports *magazine. Later a part of the famed Los Angeles Lakers "Showtime" teams, "Coop" returned to Albuquerque and coached the Albuquerque Thunderbirds in the NBA's D-League. Courtesy Gary Herron.*

> "
>
> **I'll never forget my biggest night [his 50-point game] in Lobo basketball. Before that game, I was having a cold coming on—I was feeling bad. The rim looked like a 50-gallon drum, and everything was perfect that night.**
>
> —Marvin Johnson (1976–78); March 2, 1978; UNM 111, CSU 88

It had been a stormy season for "Stormin' Norman." There had been a mutiny within the Lobo ranks, and on March 1, 1976, six of the black players on the squad quit and said they would not return to UNM if Ellenberger remained as the head man. Of course, he stayed. That boycott produced one of the more memorable wins in Lobo history. Don Haskins's UTEP Miners came to the Pit on March 6 looking to roll a UNM team with a depleted roster. UNM had retained one starter and took to the Pit floor with a starting lineup that combined for a 13.8 scoring average.

The Miners were expected to mop up the floor with the Lobos. It didn't happen. The Lobos fell behind by 12 points early, then rallied to a 56–49 lead with 3:56 left to play and held on for a 59–58 win. The Pit went nuts. Steve Davis and Dan Davis (not related) combined to score 42 points.

Earlier that season, UNM played in front of what may have been more than 20,000 fans in an 80–73 loss to UNLV. The Pit had become the place to be in Albuquerque—the watering hole for a community looking to embrace a winner.

The Lobos celebrate in their locker room after beating Wyoming 93–74 on March 4, 1978, in the WAC championship game. Courtesy UNM Athletics.

Ellenberger lost some talent off his 1975–1976 team, but he went back on the JuCo trail and brought in two of the better Lobos ever: Michael Cooper and Marvin Johnson. This team was raw and at times undisciplined on defense and shot selection, but it was athletic and it could score. The Lobos came out of the gates in 1976–1977 to score 121 points in their opener against Highlands and hit 103 in a loss at New Mexico State. These Lobos scored 90 points or more 12 times and ran to a 19–11 mark.

They got better. In 1977–1978, the Lobos scored 90 points or more 18 times in their first 21 games and posted a 19–2 mark. They went over 100 points 11 times. The Pit was mesmerized by this team and its potential, especially with the Pit being a host site for teams looking to advance to the NCAA Final Four.

The Lobos led the nation in scoring and ended the regular season at 24–4, going 13–1 in the WAC and running past ninth-ranked UNLV, 102–98, in Las Vegas. The Lobos went into the NCAA first round in Tempe, Arizona, only needing a win over no-name Cal State Fullerton to advance to the West Regional—in

the Pit. But to everyone's surprise, including no doubt some Titans fans, the Lobos were dispatched from the tournament after a 90–85 loss. Ellenberger was runner-up in Coach of the Year balloting by the US Basketball Writers Association; Michael Cooper was named to that organization's first team. (Arkansas narrowly beat underrated Fullerton in the regional finals and advanced to the Final Four.)

The Lobos of 1978–1979 did not have Cooper or Johnson (who scored 50 Pit points on March 2, 1978, vs. Colorado State); they went 19–10 and fell back into the NIT. Ellenberger got a raise of $2,300 in July of 1979 to form a base salary of $37,300.

The Lobo community was excited about the run-and-gun talent that Ellenberger had stockpiled for 1978–1979. The team was loaded. But the season and expectations crumbled when the FBI stormed into the Pit on November 28, 1979, in the first phase of a transcript-rigging scandal known as "Lobogate."

It all fell apart quickly for Ellenberger and his chief recruiter, Manny Goldstein, and nine players were ruled ineligible. Ellenberger was fired on December 17,

"

I'll never forget the UTEP game when Haskins came to the Pit. We had some players, unfortunately, who walked off for us. I got my debut to play and you get moments in your life—Steve Davis and Dan Davis and David Otero, who has since passed away—and I had probably the most memorable moment of my life playing basketball.

—Steve Davis (1974–1777); the Lobos lost the game, 68–67

Coach Norm Ellenberger and his last Lobo team, posing before the infamous 1979–1980 season. Courtesy UNM Athletics.

and what remained of the UNM roster was handed over to an assistant, Charlie Harrison. (UNM did a quick search and pulled Gary Colson out of semi-retirement, but Harrison did the on-court coaching.)

NCAA investigators determined that Lobos Andre Logan, Larry Belin, Larry Hubbard, Paul Roby, and Larry Tarrance had received credit for classes they had never taken in December 1979, or at the very least had been issued phony transcripts from colleges they never attended. Yet another Lobo, Craig Gilbert, had been previously suspended after transcript problems had been discovered. In all there were 34 NCAA violations.

Ellenberger, tried on federal and state charges, including mail fraud and filing false public vouchers, was acquitted of the federal charges but convicted on 21 state counts. His presiding judge at the state trial declined to impose a jail sentence, noting that Ellenberger was but one cog in what had become a highly competitive world of college athletics and that he was being prosecuted for trying to satisfy the school's, along with fans', demand that he produce a winning basketball program.

Ellenberger never had a collegiate head coaching job after his downfall at UNM. He coached the Albuquerque Silvers for two seasons; that Continental Basketball Association team played its games at the Albuquerque Civic Auditorium. He also coached the Albuquerque Energee (1980), a professional women's team in the Duke City. And Ellenberger also had a stint as an assistant for Tim Floyd when he coached the Chicago Bulls. He even spent time coaching high school basketball teams in the Midwest. In 1986 former rival and longtime friend Don Haskins hired Ellenberger as his lead assistant at UTEP, where he would coach for four years. After that, "Stormin' Norman" became the lead assistant for Bobby Knight for 10 seasons (1990–2000).

In a story in the *Albuquerque Journal* in 2013, Ellenberger said he had no excuses for the way his time at UNM ended and that he held no grudges. "It truly was a wonderful experience," he told the city's morning newspaper. "When I left there, part of me stayed there. I've got some really good friends there and a lot of great memories."

Sadly for Lobo fans, Ellenberger died in his sleep in November 2015 in his cabin in Watersmeet, Michigan, at the age of 83, from a series of heart ailments.

Best Memories

- **January 17, 1976:** A record 19,452 fans show up, but the UNLV Runnin' Rebels pull off an 80–73 victory.

- **March 6, 1976:** Steve Davis hits the game-winning free throw with 0:04 to play, finishing with 22 points, as the Lobos beat UTEP 59–58. UNM had four African American players quit the team earlier in the week, and fans were calling for Ellenberger's firing.

- **March 2, 1978:** Marvin "Automatic" Johnson scores 50 points in a 111–88 rout of Colorado State. Johnson played 31 minutes and was 21-of-27 from the field and 8-of-10 at the foul line. Earlier that season, Johnson had notched a school record with 46 points in a game; after a 32-point performance in his next game, *Sports Illustrated* named him its Player of the Week.

- **February 26, 1978:** Five Lobos score in double figures as UNM sets what was then an arena-scoring record with a 129–98 victory over Arizona. Russell Saunders led the way with 29 points.

Charlie Harrison (1979–1980; 6–22)

Well-traveled, Harrison began his coaching career in 1971, when he went to Indiana University and served two years as a graduate assistant coach on Bobby Knight's team, where he met future Lobos coach Dave Bliss. Later he was on Bliss's staff at Oklahoma in 1975–1976. When he arrived at UNM, prior to the 1979–1980 season, he was filling a vacancy that became available when assistant John Whisenant stepped down to enter private business. ("Whiz" had been the interim coach when Ellenberger was suspended in November 1979.)

Summoned to be the head coach when Ellenberger was dismissed in December 1979, Harrison had only four scholarship players left on the team. As former Lobo beat writer Dennis Latta wrote in the 1983 Final Four supplement in the *Albuquerque Journal*, "The Lobos played their 1978–79 basketball season with walk-ons, managers and two scholarship players. A wide receiver (Derwin Williams) on a full football scholarship started for UNM's basketball team."

What to do? Harrison organized a tryout, open to UNM students. It didn't help much; UNM added a few walk-ons and completed the season with a 6–22 record. There were two four-game losing streaks and two five-game skids.

Kenny Page, who transferred to UNM from Ohio State after the 1977–1978 season, was a bright spot, as he scored 35 or more points seven times. In December of 1979, Page scored 47 points, and he still owns the WAC's single-game scoring average of 28.0 points per game. (Despite playing just two seasons, Page ranks 16th all-time in scoring at UNM with 1,387 points.)

Harrison and his players didn't go unappreciated, though, with fans understanding the hardships incurred. "I saw a lot of tears shed by a lot of grown men," Charlie Harrison later told the *New York Times*.

Following his season as interim head coach, with Gary Colson named the new head coach, Harrison took an assistant men's basketball coaching position at Iowa State University (1980–1982); he was later the head men's basketball coach at East Carolina University (1982–1987).

Gary Colson (1980–1988; 146–106)

According to the 1980–1981 UNM media guide, "Perhaps nowhere in college basketball could athletic director John Bridgers have found a more highly respected, moral individual with a winning history that stretches over 21 years. Gary Colson was just what the doctor ordered."

Bridgers found Colson relaxing on his houseboat off the shore of Malibu after a 22–10 season as head coach at Pepperdine University. Assuring Lobo fans that Charlie Harrison was in charge for what remained of the 1979–1980 season, Colson hit the recruiting trail.

His coaching staff was made up of one of his players from his days as head coach at Valdosta State (in Georgia), Bob Lamphier; Dave Edmonds, also a Georgia connection; Scott Duncan, who had spent two seasons as an assistant at Cleveland State; and former Lobo Jim Williams, who was coming off the best of his four seasons at UNM, starting 26 of 28 games and averaging 10.7 points and 7.4 rebounds as a senior (1979–1980).

It was slow going for Colson, as his first three seasons didn't produce any winning records, although UNM was 14–14 in 1981–1982. But in his fourth season at the helm, he matched Ellenberger's season-best 24 wins and led the Lobos to third place in the WAC in 1983–1984. After 19- and 17-win seasons the next two years, Colson's 1986–1987 team won 25 games and tied for third in the WAC.

Despite 22 wins in 1987–1988, Athletic Director John Koenig decided it was time for a change. Colson resigned under pressure on April 26, paid (according to the *Albuquerque Tribune*) around $200,000 to do so. He had two years remaining on his contract. "We appreciate the accomplishments of Gary Colson and his staff in bringing our basketball program to prominence both academically and athletically," Koenig said. "His student athletes have an excellent graduation rate."

Fortunately for the Lobos and their fans, two players—Rob Robbins, who had red-shirted in Colson's final season, and Australian center Luc Longley—who said they'd chosen UNM because of Colson decided to remain Lobos. Highly recruited Matt Othick decided to go elsewhere, heading to Tucson to play for the University of Arizona.

Colson headed west, landing at Fresno State, a Lobos foe in the WAC from 1990–1995.

UNM, according to Koenig, had a list of 23 names as possible replacements for Colson, including Gene Keady of Purdue, Jerry Pimm of Cal-Santa Barbara, and the man they ultimately hired.

I'll never forget my first game in the Pit, coaching. Someone asked if I was nervous and I said, 'No, I am terrified.'

—Gary Colson (head coach, 1980–1988); November 28, 1980; Colorado 75, UNM 65

I'll never forget, as a fan, when Royce [Olney] beat up on Andre Miller and came down and made that 3. [And then, as a player,] making the shot versus Air Force at the buzzer. We were down by one—the buzzer went off as the ball was in the air.

—Nelson Franse (1982–1984); February 20, 1984; UNM 49, AFA 48

High-scoring newcomer Kenny Page (number 10), a transfer from Ohio State, was the perfect player to place on the 1980–1981 media guide. Courtesy Gary Herron.

(left to right) Lobos Wallace Williams (number 11), Phil Smith (number 12), Kenny Page (number 10), and Jerome Henderson (number 44) in UNM's 72–60 win over Charleston on December 22, 1980. Courtesy Gary Herron.

Gary Colson's first team, the 1980–1981 Lobos, in their preseason team photo. Courtesy UNM Athletics.

Top: Kenny Page (number 10) drives the baseline in a 1981 game at the Pit. Thirty-five years later, he's still remembered as one of the best Lobos of all time. Courtesy UNM Athletics.

Bottom: Where "Make It Happen" had been the slogan in 1977–1978, the 1982–1983 season was dubbed "Year of the Lobo" on bumper stickers seen around the Duke City. Courtesy Gary Herron.

Tim Fullmer (number 34) played for UNM for two seasons (1981–1983). Here, he battles to get a shot off against UNLV's Larry Anderson. The Lobos won that January 9, 1982, game, 72–70. Courtesy Gary Herron.

Top: The Lobos (in white) beat visiting New Mexico State 57–51 in the Pit on December 22, 1983, five days after a 67–60 loss to the Aggies in Las Cruces. Courtesy Gary Herron.

Bottom: Lobos guard Phil Smith at the foul line in a 1981 contest. Courtesy Gary Herron.

That's T. J. Drake trying to get the attention of an official, but he's outnumbered by Aggies trying to get a call at the December 22, 1983, Lobos-Aggies game in the Pit. Courtesy Gary Herron.

The 1983–1984 Lobos' team photo, taken at the start of coach Gary Colson's fourth season. Courtesy UNM Athletics.

Lobo guard Kelvin Scarborough keeps an eye on an opponent near the baseline. Courtesy Gary Herron.

I'll never forget when I made my first dunk versus Wyoming, when about 18,000 people came to their feet [freshman season], but my greatest memory in the Pit wasn't basketball at all, it was coming down after the game to sign autographs—to see 2,000 people down there waiting was amazing—that was my whole career.

—Kelvin Scarborough (1983–1987);
February 16, 1984;
UNM 62, Wyoming 54

Guard Kelvin Scarborough goes in for a layup in the team's 103–71 rout of Morgan State on November 23, 1984. Courtesy UNM Athletics.

Forward Alan Dolensky (1980–1984) takes an arm to the face while going up for a shot against the Utes. Courtesy Gary Herron.

"

I'll never forget the Georgetown game. I remember Patrick Ewing was hurt and they didn't want to play with him; he had a hurt thumb. . . . It was a four- or six-point game the whole way through. We were down six, we get a steal, George Scott drives the middle and Ewing just throws it out. . . . Then we ended up losing, but that was a chance we had to win. They were ranked in the top-five. I will never forget that game; that was one of the greatest games I've seen in the Pit.

—Yvonne Sanchez (UNM women's basketball coach, 2011–2016);
December 22, 1984; Georgetown 69, UNM 61

A full-house crowd of 18,018 was on hand January 25, 1986, to see a 71–70 overtime loss to UTEP. Courtesy UNM Athletics.

Coming off a 24–11 campaign in 1983–1984, the 1984–1985 team hammed it up at its team photo session. Courtesy UNM Athletics.

The 1986–1987 Lobos team photo. The squad won 25 games but lost its last two games, 64–62 to Wyoming in the WAC championship game in the Pit and 85–82 to Oregon State in the NIT, also played in the Pit. Courtesy UNM Athletics.

"

I'll never forget our game against Wyoming with only 7 or 8 seconds left. We fouled Wyoming's point guard Sean Dent, who wasn't a very good free shooter. He missed the front end of a 1-and-1. I got the rebound out to Mike Winters, who dribbled past half-court and passed it back to me for a jump shot, but before I shot it I took a step back behind the 3-point line—not needing a 3, it was just instinct—booyah! It went in and the Pit was wild. [I still remember] my teammates, coaches, and all the fans celebrating.

—Hunter Greene (1983–88); February 26, 1987;
UNM 92, Wyoming 89

Best Memories

- **December 21, 1984:** A crowd of 16,742—not the biggest of the season—watches senior George Scott drop in 20 points against the Arizona Wildcats in a memorable 59–58 Pit win.

- **December 22, 1984:** One night later, a crowd of 17,029 watches Patrick Ewing and the first-ranked Georgetown Hoyas beat the Lobos 69–61, pulling away from a narrow 60–57 lead with 3:48 left in the game. The Hoyas held what appeared to be a safe, 17-point lead at halftime.

- **January 25, 1986:** Some moronic Lobo fan tosses a paper cup in the area of UTEP's Wayne Campbell, who was shooting foul shots at the time. Although he missed, the referees gave him another shot because of the egregious paper cup toss, and Campbell sank both to help the Miners pull off a 71–70 win in overtime. Coach Gary Colson termed it the toughest loss of his career.

- **January 10, 1987:** Hunter Greene leads all starters in double-digits with a career-best 32 points as UNM scorches BYU 102–89 in front of 18,046 rabid fans. Kelly Graves adds 20 points and seven-footer Rob Loeffel scores 213 points and grabs 14 rebounds. The victory gives UNM a share of second place, with BYU and UTEP, in the WAC.

- **January 2, 1988:** Playing with a fever, Hunter Greene swats away a last-second shot by Sean Elliott, and UNM pulls off a 61–59 upset of first-ranked Arizona in front of 18,000 or so fans and a national audience tuned in to ESPN. Freshman Jimmy Rogers came off the bench to lead UNM with 15 points, a performance termed "awesome" by Colson.

After Colson set sail and before Dave Bliss was ultimately hired, UNM fans were intrigued that "The General," Bobby Knight, might be their team's next head coach.

That May the *Albuquerque Tribune* reported that negotiations between Knight and UNM were underway, with Knight seeking a five-year contract with salary and other job-related income worth close to $250,000 annually, plus a home in Albuquerque.

The source said Knight had approached UNM Athletic Director John Koenig about the job. Another source said the two met to discuss the job one weekend in Louisville. Knight's base salary at Indiana was $95,400 a year, and his overall income was estimated as high as $500,000 a year, including money from a lucrative summer camp.

Knight, then 47, arrived in Albuquerque and spent much of an evening at the home of UNM President Gerald May, where he, May, and Koenig had dinner and discussed the Lobo job. A meeting with Lobo basketball players was set for the next afternoon, when Koenig was expected to inform the players of the status of the search to replace Gary Colson.

At the time, Knight was under fire at Indiana University because of several incidents that transpired during his tenure with the Hoosiers. Needless to say, Knight didn't get the job at UNM, although one of his acquaintances did—a guy The General suggested.

Dave Bliss (1988–1999; 246–108)

A former assistant to Knight at West Point and Indiana, Bliss was once termed by Knight as the smartest assistant he'd ever had. An All-East and All-Ivy league guard in basketball while at Cornell, where he graduated in 1965, Bliss was drafted into the US Army in 1967. Knight, the coach at Army, remembered Bliss from his days at Cornell and hired him to be an assistant, and that led Bliss, who spent two years with The General, to decide that coaching was his calling.

From 1971 to 1975, Bliss worked for Knight at Indiana University, then got his first head coaching job at the University of Oklahoma (1975–1980). He followed that up with the head coaching job at Southern Methodist University (1980–1988). When the job at UNM opened, Knight was a proponent for Bliss, saying, "The University of New Mexico

Once in a while, you can find a "Lobo Basketball is Bliss" pin online or at a local flea market. Courtesy Gary Herron.

"

I'll never forget my first year, when Charlie Thomas made a free throw to put us up by one against Hawaii. Nine seconds were left—we beat them and we share the WAC championship. They go down to the other end, a guy takes a shot, Luc tips the ball and it goes straight into the basket.

—Dave Bliss (head coach, 1988–1999); March 4, 1988; Hawaii 71, UNM 70

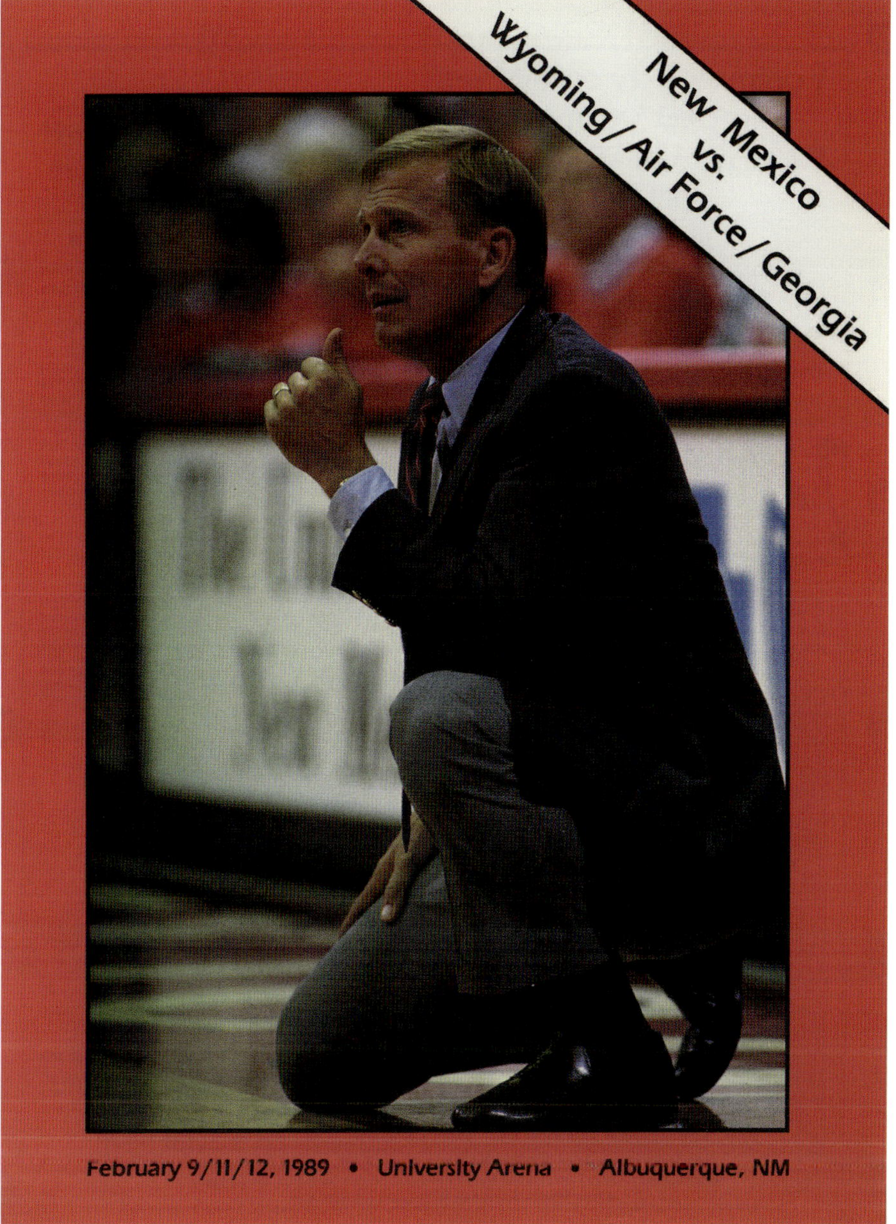

basketball job is one of the best in the nation. By hiring a coach like Dave Bliss, [UNM] is putting together a blend of the best with the best."

The Lobos, 22–14 in Colson's last season, hadn't been to the postseason in a decade. That changed in Bliss's first season—and for the next 10. That's right: 11 for 11.

Bliss became the rookie head coach with the most wins in UNM history, going 22–11 in his debut season, tying for second in the WAC, and coming within an eyelash of winning its first conference title since 1978.

The Lobos finished second in the nation in field-goal percentage, canning a school- and WAC-record 54.5 percent of their 2-point shots. Charlie Thomas and Luc Longley earned second-team All-WAC laurels; Rob Robbins and Darrell McGee received honorable mention.

The clock ticks down the final seconds of the Lobos' exciting 61–59 victory over first-ranked Arizona on January 2, 1988. In a list compiled in the summer of 1999 by a blue-ribbon panel of writers and fans, this was voted the number one game of all time. Courtesy UNM Athletics.

The Lobos won back-to-back NIT games in the Pit, 91–76 over Santa Clara and 86–69 over Pepperdine, before St. Louis ended hopes of traveling to New York City and the semifinals, beating them 66–65.

Twenty-win seasons became the norm: Bliss led the Lobos to records of 20–14 in 1989–1990, 20–10 in 1990–1991, 20–13 in 1991–1992, 24–7 in 1992–1993, and 23–8 in 1993–1994. Also becoming the norm were one-and-done appearances in the NCAA: a 67–54 loss to Oklahoma State in 1991; an 82–68 loss to George Washington in 1993; and a 57–54 setback to Virginia in 1994.

After a 15–15 no-postseason campaign in 1994–1995, UNM was back to winning 20 or more games, going 28–5 in 1995–1996 and winning the WAC Tournament—finally with a first-round NCAA win, 69–48, over Kansas State before a 73–62 loss to Georgetown.

Bliss's final three seasons featured 24 or more wins: 25–8, with a 59–55 NCAA win over Old Dominion before a 64–63 loss to Louisville, in 1996–1997; 24–8 with a 79–62 NCAA win over Butler before a 56–46 loss to Syracuse in 1997–1998; and 25–9, capped by a 61–59 victory over Missouri in the first round of the NCAA before a 78–56 loss to third-ranked University of Connecticut (UConn) in 1998–1999.

Who better to feature on this program at the tail end of the 1990–1991 season than outgoing senior Luc Longley, with photos from his freshman and senior seasons? The Lobos won both of these games, by the way—92–55 over the Falcons and 68–62 over the 13th-ranked Utes. Courtesy Gary Herron.

The Lobos celebrated 25 years of playing home games in the Pit in the 1991–1992 season, and they beat Tennessee State 107–59 on December 21, 1991. Courtesy Gary Herron.

For several seasons during Dave Bliss's tenure as head coach, trading cards of UNM basketball players and coaches—and even broadcaster Mike Powers—were available to collectors. These are from the 1993–1994 season. Courtesy Gary Herron.

"

I'll never forget when UNM was up in regulation by nine with like 20 seconds to go. We put New Mexico State on the foul line; they get the offensive rebound because they can't shoot free throws and they kick it out for a 3. Then they get a steal on the inbounds and hit another."

—J. J. Griego (1989–1990, 1991–1994);
December 11, 1993; NMSU 112, UNM 104, double overtime

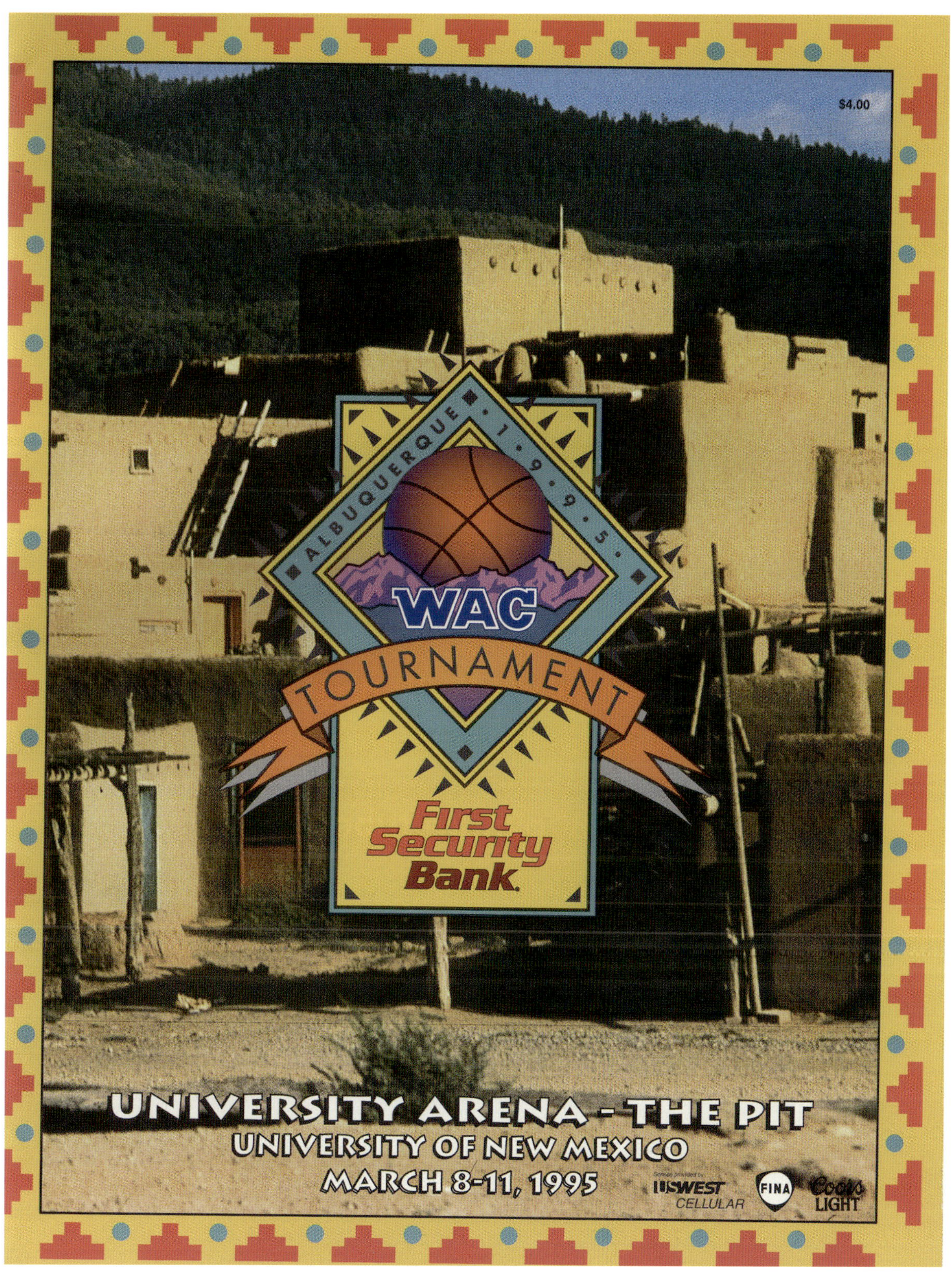

The Pit hosted the 1995 WAC Tournament. After a 63–56 victory over Wyoming, 22nd-ranked Utah defeated the Lobos 86–50. There was no postseason appearance in the 1994–1995 season, when UNM compiled a 15–15 record. Courtesy Gary Herron.

Coach Dave Bliss and the 1995–1996 team, which went on to win the WAC Tournament and an NCAA Tournament game, 59–55, over Old Dominion, before a season-ending 64–63 heartbreaking loss to Louisville. Courtesy Gary Herron.

The 1995–1996 Lobo team. Front row (left to right): Manager Brian Wade, Cedric Hopkins, David Gibson, Steve Lewis, Coach Dave Bliss, Charles Smith, Royce Olney, Kavossy Franklin, and Manager Ellis Dawson. Back row (left to right): Administrative Assistant J. J. DeTemple, Assistant Coach Doug Ash, Clayton Shields, Shawn Simpson, Chris Paddock, Daniel Santiago, Ben Baum, Marty Cotwright, Kenny Thomas, Greg Schornstein, and Assistant Coach Tony Benford. Courtesy Gary Herron.

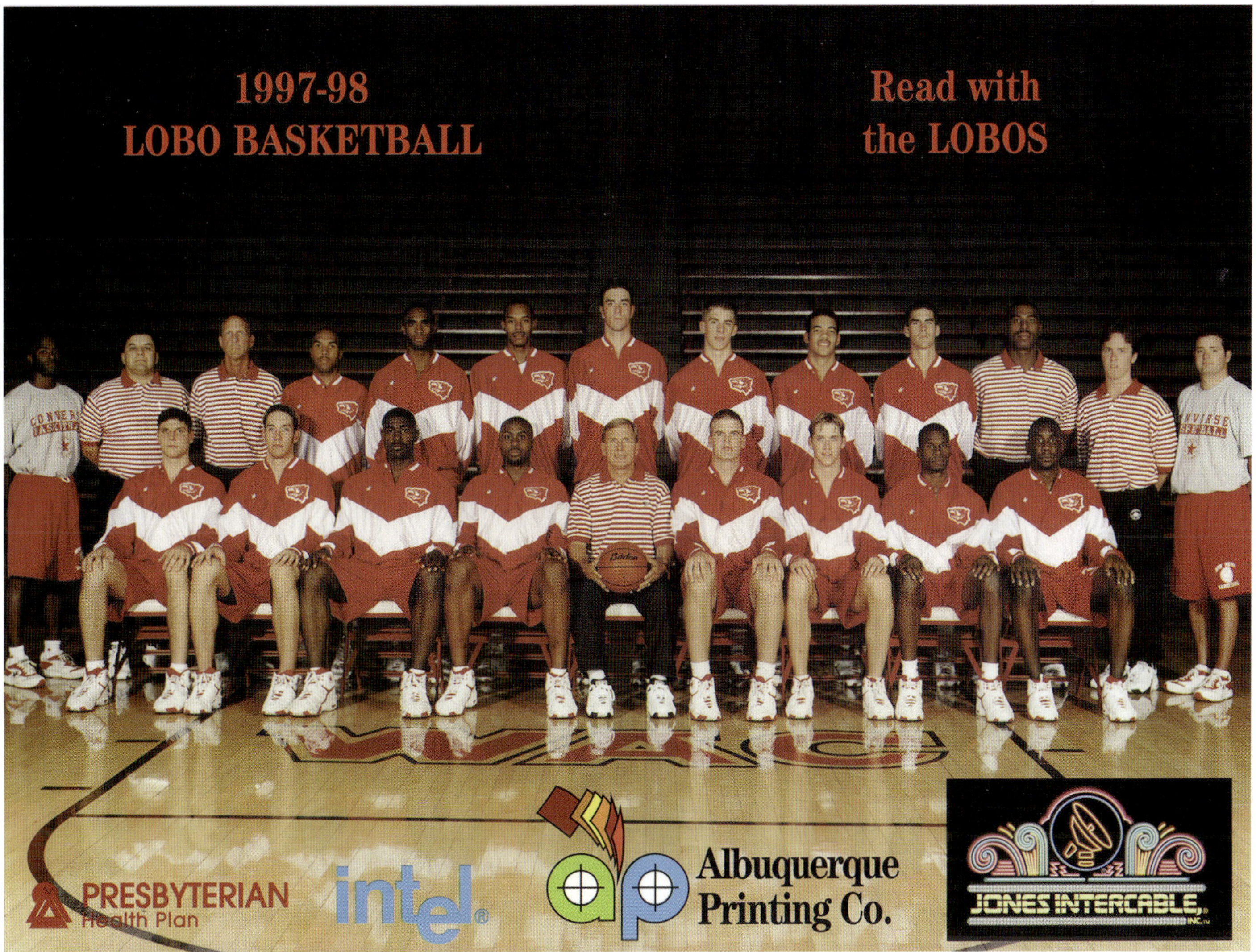

The 1997–1998 Lobos finished 24–8, which included a 56–51 loss to UNLV in the WAC championship game, then a 79–62 victory over Butler in an NCAA first-round game in Louisville. The season then ended with a 79–62 NCAA loss to Syracuse, also in Louisville. Courtesy Gary Herron.

"

I'll never forget when the WAC Tournament was held in the Pit. The Lobos and Fresno State were playing in a semifinal game that lasted three overtimes, with UNM winning, 104–98. It was a very draining, emotional game, with the defining moment coming in the second overtime, and the Lobos down by three with three seconds to play, when Charles Smith was fouled shooting a 3-pointer. He made all three free throws and the Lobos went on to win the game.

—Paul Opperman (longtime statistician at the scorer's table);
March 8, 1996; UNM 104, Fresno State 99, triple overtime

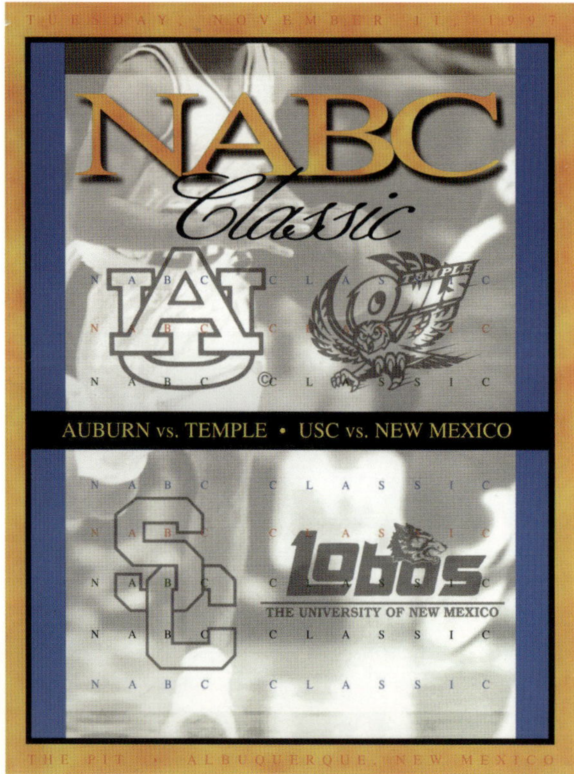

The National Association of Basketball Coaches held its annual "Classic" at the Pit in November 1997. The Lobos beat USC 98–76 in their matchup. Courtesy Gary Herron.

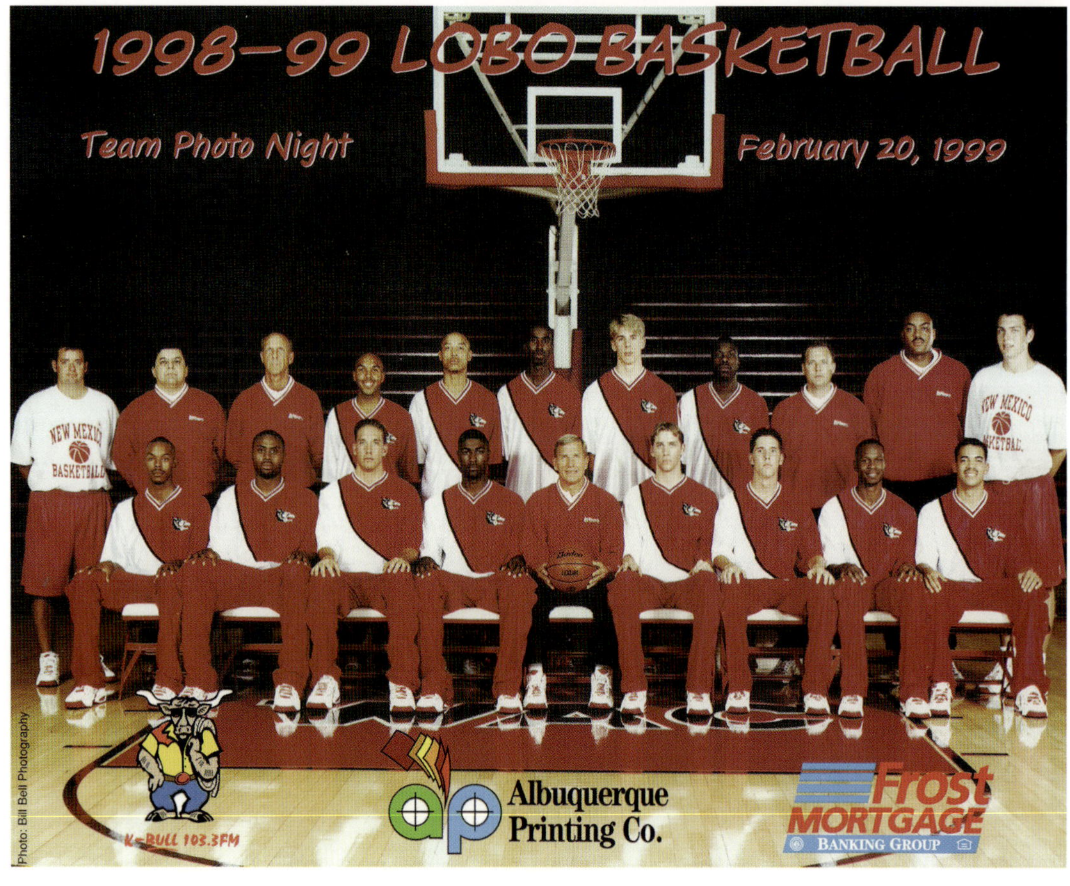

The 1998–1999 season was an encore of the previous season, this time with a WAC title tilt loss to Utah, followed by a 61–59 NCAA victory in Denver over Missouri, followed by a 78–56 loss to UConn. It was coach Dave Bliss's final season. Courtesy Gary Herron.

Action in the Pit during the Lobos' days in the WAC. Courtesy UNM Athletics.

More Pit action during the Lobos' WAC days, taken from a vantage point at the southwest corner of the arena. Courtesy UNM Athletics.

An aerial shot of action on the Pit floor, shot from high above the south end. Courtesy UNM Athletics.

Top: Remember when people sent postcards, back in the days before e-mail? No doubt some visiting Albuquerque sent their friends this one, issued when the seating capacity was 14,831 fans. *Courtesy Gary Herron.*

Bottom: The Little Point Guard: The Greg Brown Story (A Mother's Perspective) *was written by Mary Brown, mother of the 1994 Frances Pomeroy Naismith winner. The book is described as "a motivational book for anyone who has ever had a dream." Courtesy Gary Herron.*

Despite his success with the Lobos, Bliss—twice the conference's Coach of the Year—resigned and headed to Baylor, where he doubled his salary.

His 102 wins (with just 30 losses) in his final four seasons were surpassed by only nine other institutions, led by Kentucky (132 wins); the list included such perennial basketball powerhouses as Kansas, Duke, Cincinnati, North Carolina, and Arizona.

As Bliss departed, UNM had been in the postseason 15 times in the previous 16 seasons and had gone 16 seasons without a losing record, bettered by only five schools: UCLA, University of North Carolina (UNC), Syracuse, Indiana, and Oklahoma. Bliss still leads UNM in postseason victories (7 NIT wins, 4 NCAA wins), although he also has 11 postseason losses.

Bliss's downfall is documented in his 2015 book, *Fall to Grace: The Climb, Collapse, and Comeback of Coach Dave Bliss*. Most Lobo fans are aware of the tragedy that befell former Lobo Patrick Dennehy after he transferred to Baylor to play for Bliss. In a nutshell, Bliss writes, "after coaching thirty-six years at the Division I level, I committed several NCAA violations between 2002 and 2003, including personally paying the scholarships of two players. When an unrelated murder occurred involving one of the players, I panicked, and an unbelievable set of circumstances resulted in my resignation. You could say that my life spiraled out of control."

At press time, he was coaching at Southwestern Christian University in Oklahoma City.

Best Memories

- **February 23, 1991:** Maybe not a pleasant memory, but a memory nonetheless: A national TV audience was watching as the Pit was emptied out because of a bomb scare during UNM's game with UTEP. A crowd of 18,100 evacuated the building at halftime, but no device was found. The game, which started late because it was on ESPN, ended at 12:50 a.m. MST. UNM won 80-74.

- **December 11, 1993:** Before a capacity crowd, UNM squandered a 15-point lead in the second half of a game against New Mexico State, and despite Greg Brown's career-high 34 points—15 in overtime—lost 112-104 in double overtime. The thriller left UNM with its first loss in 62 games in which it had scored 100 or more points. Twenty-three turnovers didn't help the Lobos, who shot 42 times from behind the 3-point arc.

- **March 8, 1996:** Charles "Spider" Smith hits three consecutive free throws to force a third overtime and UNM outlasts Fresno State 104-99 in a WAC Tournament semifinal game. David Gibson's two free throws were the final points in a game that fans ranked the fifth-best game in Pit history.

- **March 9, 1996:** Freshman Kenny Thomas pours in 30 points, including 23 of the Lobos' first 32 points, and hauls down 17 rebounds to help the Lobos beat 10th-ranked Utah 64-60 in the WAC Tournament championship game.

- **February 1, 1998:** Royce Olney swipes the ball from Utah's Andre Miller en route to nailing a 25-footer with 4.7 seconds left to play in UNM's thrilling 77-74 win over Coach Rick Majerus and the previously unbeaten Utes. The victory left the Lobos and Utes tied for first place in the WAC's Mountain Division and extended UNM's home-court winning streak to 38 games. "My favorite game," Bliss recalled in 2016. (A footnote: WAC Commissioner Karl Benson later said a foul should have been called on Olney. "It was a foul on Olney in our review of the film," Benson said. "Had that play happened two minutes into the game, it certainly wouldn't have had the magnitude it had at the end of the game.")

- **January 16, 1999:** The 16th-ranked Lobos upset 7th-ranked Arizona 79-78 on a buzzer-beating lay-up by Damion Walker off a pass from John Robinson II. The Lobos had trailed the Wildcats by 15 at halftime.

Chapter 4   # Making History

The 1983 Final Four

Almost everybody who was alive and living in Albuquerque can tell you what happened in March of 1983 that put the Duke City—and the Pit—on the map: the NCAA Final Four.

If it wasn't significant, why would ESPN create a memorable "30 for 30" documentary on North Carolina State's (NC State's) run to the championship? This "Cardiac Pack" won seven of its last nine games after trailing with a minute left in the game.

And, speaking of a run, who can forget third-year Wolfpack coach Jim Valvano circling the Pit floor after Lorenzo Charles's buzzer-beating dunk—off what was either an "air ball" or an alley-oop pass from Dereck Whittenburg—beat favored Houston and its "Phi Slama Jama" crew?

When asked about it in the postgame press conference, Whittenburg responded, "I wasn't thinking about it. Like I said, it was a pass, to tell the truth." (Or was it?) He continued,

> When I got the ball, I couldn't see the backboard or the clock, so I couldn't see the time. . . . I couldn't see no time, so I was taking a shot at the basket—I didn't realize how far I was (away), or where I was, I just wanted to get it to the basket. I was looking for it to go in, that's all I was trying

Left: A commemorative Final Four poster available throughout Albuquerque in 1983. Courtesy Gary Herron.

Right: A Final Four pin sold in the Duke City before the NCAA Championship. They're still found occasionally on eBay. Courtesy Gary Herron.

to think. When I looked up, I seen Lorenzo had grabbed it and dunked it. Time just ran out; I didn't know happened. I looked at coach; he looked at me. We didn't know what happened. . . . That was the end of the ballgame.

Keep in mind, this was several seasons before the 3-point shot was added to college basketball. There was no shot clock, either. And the field then was made up of 52 teams.

Making their way to the Duke City were:

- Second-ranked Louisville (32–3), on a 15-game winning streak and coached by Denny Crum, and led on the court by brothers Scooter and Rodney McCray
- First-ranked Houston (30–2), led by the *Associated Press*'s Coach of the Year, Guy Lewis, and acquiring the "Jama" moniker for the 62 slam dunks by seven-foot Nigerian Akeem Olajuwon;

The North Carolina State media guide made available to the media before the Final Four. Courtesy Gary Herron.

A $20 ticket to the Saturday semifinals. Courtesy Gary Herron.

6' 7" Clyde Drexler, with 52 dunks; and Michael Young and Larry Micheaux, who combined for another 32 dunks (how could the Cougars *not* be the favorites?); the Cougars hadn't lost a game since mid-December

- Overachieving Georgia (24–9), led by 6' 5" guard Vern Fleming, averaging 17 points a game, coached by Hugh Durham and making its first postseason tournament
- NC State (24–10), led by fiery Jim Valvano, who said, "Every time we win a big game we party. We've been partying a lot lately."

That wasn't Valvano's best line: on Friday he told the media, "Last night, we had our first bed check in 16 years. All the beds were there."

There would be more of that for the Wolfpack, which first had to get past Georgia in a semifinal game at the Pit at 1:39 p.m. on Saturday, April 2. Fans were excited for the opportunity to see two games on that day, as evidenced by an estimated 10,000 fans—a larger crowd than Houston saw at most of its regular-season games—which turned out Friday to see the four teams practice.

The *Albuquerque Tribune* polled "those in the know" for their picks of who would win: Mayor Harry Kinney, UNM point guard Phil Smith, and UNM football coach Joe Lee Dunn all went with Houston. So did Albuquerque Dukes general manager Pat McKernan, Georgetown coach John Thompson, and Alabama coach Wimp Sanderson. Former UNM coach Norm Ellenberger, coaching the Continental Basketball Association's Albuquerque Silvers, liked Louisville. His successor with the Lobos, Gary Colson, picked Houston.

The NCAA had souvenirs for fans going to the games: a long-sleeve red jersey or a short-sleeve gray-blue T-shirt cost $11; you could get a white pullover sweater for $20; and a red, white, and blue Final Four baseball cap went for $8.

Houston's Michael Young (number 42) goes in for a baseline layup in the first half of the national championship game. Courtesy Gary Herron.

The Pit had undergone changes for its showcase event: a requirement by the NCAA was extra lights, so 64 additional lights were installed to enhance TV coverage, at a cost of $15,000. That added an estimated 40 percent of footcandle power.

Press benches—400 to 500 media members covered the event—were built, resulting in a loss of 734 seats. Fourteen rows, in sections 19, 20, and 21 on the west side, accommodated the media; the front rows on the north and south ends were reserved for photojournalists. On the east side, where "press row" existed, a deck was built for statisticians and scorekeepers, per the NCAA. Four camera mounts were built for CBS's coverage: one on the ramp, one in the mezzanine, one on the

A ticket for the championship game cost only $20—what a bargain, eh? Courtesy Gary Herron.

A poster brought into the Pit by a Wolfpack fan, sitting in the southwest corner. Courtesy Gary Herron.

west side, and one on the northwest side. Naturally, NCAA logos—five in all—were placed on the floor, although UNM's logos remained. A new building, built on the south end of the Pit, was used for interviews with coaches and players. Tables were located within that building for writers to type and send their stories. This new building would later be used for UNM gymnastics teams.

On the morning of the semifinals, a parade—telecast on the CBS affiliate in the Duke City, KRQE-TV—began at the arena, headed east on what was then University Boulevard to Yale Avenue, and then west on Anderson Avenue to Buena Vista Drive, north on Buena Vista to Sunset Terrace, and from there, east to University Boulevard, ending in the parking lot at the Pit.

On the radio, it seemed like Duran Duran's "Hungry like the Wolf" was always playing; significant, it would turn out, when the NC State Wolfpack went on to win the title.

Once the action began Saturday afternoon, NC State didn't have any trouble beating Georgia in the first semifinal, a 67–60 victory. The Bulldogs shot just 35.1 percent from the field and never led. Dereck Whittenburg and Thurl Bailey led the Pack offense with 20 points apiece, and Cozell McQueen hauled in 13 rebounds.

Shortly after that game ended, the two 30-win teams met, and Houston slam-dunked its way to an easy 94–81 victory over the Cardinals. Drexler and

Olajuwon (Olajuwon later changed his first name to Hakeem) had 21 points apiece, and "The Dream" blocked eight shots and pulled down a game-high 22 rebounds, 15 of which came in the decisive second half. Louisville led at halftime, 41–36.

A crowd of 17,327—less than the usual 18,018 for a packed Pit because of the large media section on the west side—attended Saturday's contests. Some had paid as much as $400 for their ducats, although tickets could be found at face value just before the first tip-off. Houston was favored by the fourth-biggest point spread in NCAA championship game history.

After the win, Valvano joked with the media: "Albuquerque is the greatest city that the Lord has ever made."

Valvano continued, "My wife is pregnant—she doesn't know it, but she's going to be—and we are going to name our kid Al B. Kerky." He also joked that he got the flu "from a Spanish dancer" on Thursday night, and he was putting off a needed hernia operation, "because I'm superstitious, until next year's NCAA Tournament."

Top: It's all over! NC State's rabid fans hail their new national champs. Courtesy Gary Herron.

Bottom: North Carolina State coach Jim Valvano (right) looks on as Dereck Whittenburg shows who the new number one is. Courtesy Gary Herron.

Head Coach Jim Valvano and his Wolfpack players show everyone who's the new number-one team in the nation on the Pit floor. Courtesy Gary Herron.

I'll never forget the NCAA championship game in 1983. Being with the Valencia County *News-Bulletin* at the time, probably the smallest of all the media covering the game, I was seated way back in the southwest corner of the Pit, right next to the N C State band. What an atmosphere!

—Gary Herron (author of *Fifty Years at the Pit*)

An ecstatic NC State head coach Jim Valvano answers a question from the media following his team's win over Houston. Courtesy Gary Herron.

Being serious, he noted his team's concern with Olajuwon and the thought that maybe NC State would let Houston try to beat them from the foul line:

Sidney (Lowe) has, you know, just been absolutely dynamite, as the three seniors—I can't say enough about them, how fortunate I am, because not only are they great players but they're better people than they are players.

I've been talking about 'the dream' for a long, long time. When I first got into coaching, I just wanted to win an NCAA championship. I wanted to be in the Final Four.

The great thing about college basketball—I'm not taking a shot at college football—is when you win the national championship, it's not by some poll [as it was before the playoff system came about]. It's done on the floor. And the great thing, too, is the NCAA Tournament [captivates] every player from every level, high school on up. . . . Everybody is [captivated] by the NCAA Tournament, because there is hope. If we don't beat Wake Forest 71–70 [in the ACC Tournament], we don't play in the NCAA Tournament.

The strategy, he said, was to keep the game "in the 50s." The final score? NC State 54, Houston 52.

So his dream was realized at the Pit.

"I told the kids we were 20 minutes away," Valvano told the media he had told his team at halftime. "For me it was 16 years; for them, however long—four years in college. It's something that you'll never forget for as long as I coach, as long as they

Another view of victorious NC State coach Jim Valvano with his players as they celebrate their 1983 national championship on the Pit floor. Courtesy Gary Herron.

play, that we will be national champions. That's what I told them, 'So just play to win the game.' Then we just couldn't put the ball in the ocean at all."

Next on his to-do list, Valvano said that memorable day, "We're gonna hang the banner up in Raleigh."

Sadly, Valvano lost his battle with cancer.

Despite his team's loss—Houston would lose again in 1984 in the Final Four in Seattle, this time to Patrick Ewing and Georgetown—Olajuwon was named the tournament's Most Outstanding Player, the last player as of 2016 to earn that title while playing for a team that didn't win the national championship.

Today in Raleigh, North Carolina, knowledgeable NC State fans will tell you the Wolfpack played five of the seven programs that held the number one ranking for at least one week during the 1982–1983 season and that the real "run" of that season occurred from January 12 through February 12, when NC State was without Whittenburg, who'd broken his foot and was out of action—and that is the only time that the team truly struggled.

In 2013, coinciding with the start of the NCAA's 75th Final Four in Atlanta, *USA Today Sports* ranked the previous 74 Final Fours. Albuquerque's great 1983 finish was ranked third, behind only the 1979 battle between Michigan State and Indiana State,

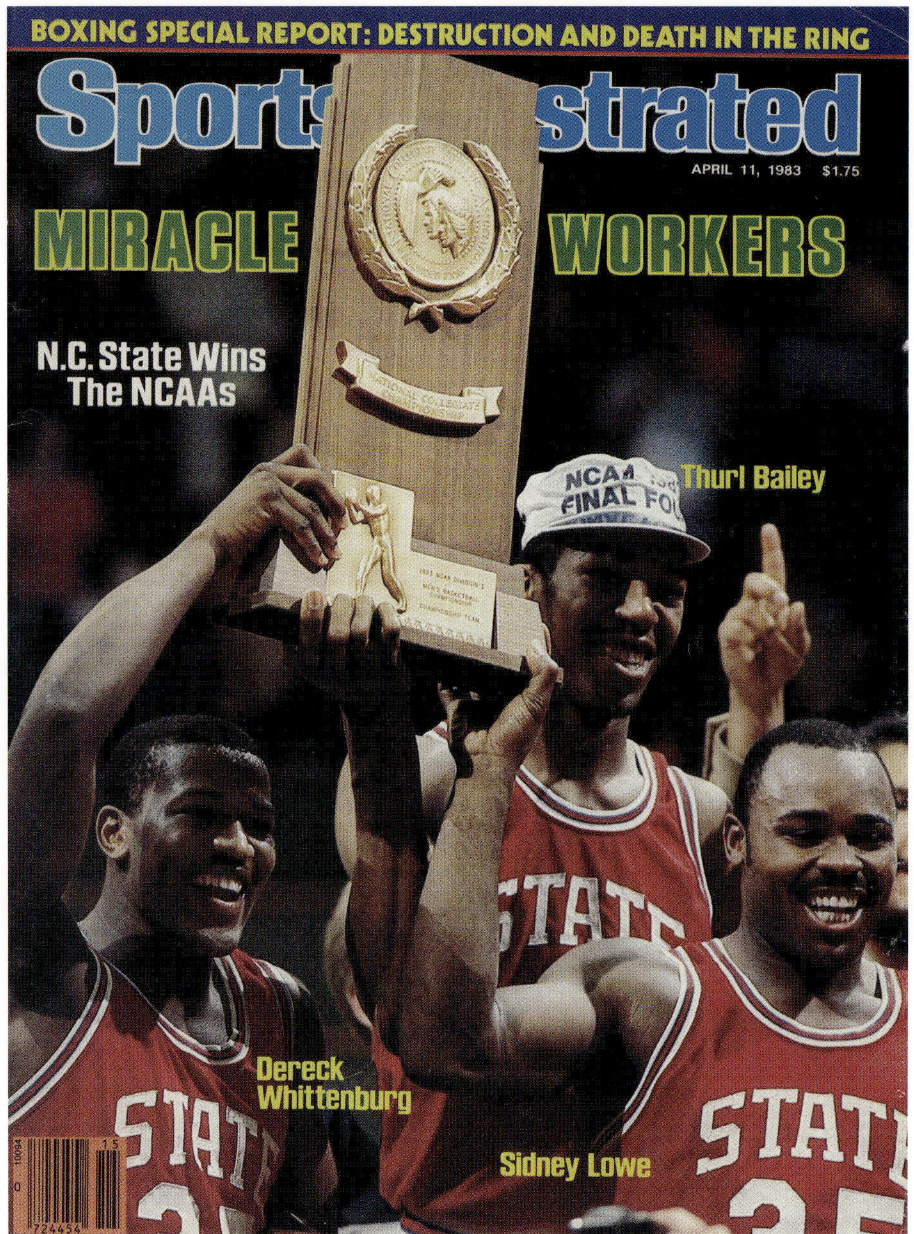

Sports Illustrated *recognizes the national champs on the cover of its April 11, 1983, issue. Courtesy Gary Herron.*

which more people remember as the showdown between Earvin "Magic" Johnson and Larry Bird, and the second-ranked memorable Texas Western (now UTEP) contest with Adolph Rupp's Kentucky, glamorized in the 2006 movie *Glory Road*.

As a postscript, many "experts" said the 2016 Final Four championship game between victorious Villanova and NC State now has the distinction of being the greatest ending in hoops history.

Right after UNC's Ryan Arcidiacono hit an off-balance 3-point shot to tie the game at 74 with 4.7 seconds left, the Wildcats' Kris Jenkins trumped the Tar Heels with a game-winning trey from NBA range.

Don Flanagan and the Women's Resurgence

If Bob King was the architect of UNM men's basketball, then Don Flanagan was the engineer for women's basketball at UNM.

Flanagan is the guy people point to when it comes to crediting the women's team for its resurgence in the mid-1990s, which came with five MWC Tournament championships and seven NCAA Tournament appearances. Flanagan has been gone for half a decade, but the program still resonates with fans.

An intense Don Flanagan eyes the action on the Pit floor. Courtesy UNM Athletics.

The 2015–2016 season marked the 17th consecutive season the UNM women were in the top 25 in attendance and the 17th consecutive year they finished at the top of the MWC. The MWC finished 7th among all the conferences in the country. The Lobos were just shy of averaging 4,000 more fans per game than the MWC average of 1,622.

In the Lobos' 17 homes games of 2015–2016, they averaged an attendance of 5,511 per game and played in front of a total of 93,683 fans inside WisePies Arena. Outside the "Power 5" conferences, the Lobos ranked second in the nation in average attendance behind national champion UConn.

That's a long way from where they'd been about 15 years before, when fans were few and far between. In the 1994–1995 campaign only eight season tickets were sold—four of them purchased by UNM President Richard Peck, Flanagan said.

UNM didn't have records available for women's teams that played in Carlisle Gym, which opened in 1928, but it's doubtful that fans "crammed Carlisle."

Former Lobo Linda (Hattox) Toppert recalled her team's games preceding Lobo men's games starting in 1974, when UNM lost its first game in the Pit 79–45 to Gallup on January 10, 1974.

Prior to the rebirth of the program in 1991 and to the unbounded success that came after Flanagan arrived on the scene, UNM's women's teams were coached by Kathy Marpe (Intermountain Conference, 1974–1980; a record of 79–58) and Doug Hoselton (High Country Conference, 1980–1987; 89–105).

Key players "back in the day" were Jean Rostermundt, who led the team in scoring for four seasons (1976–1980) and finished her career with 1,541 points; Yvonne McKinnon (1981–1985; 1,416 career points); Alison Foote (1981–1985; 1,672 points); Tracy Satran (1984–1987; 1,027 points); and rebounding maven Carol Moreland (1975–1980; career rebounding leader with 982, which included 36 in a single game!). All five also grabbed more

than 500 rebounds in their careers; McKinnon's 35 points against Adams State on February 19, 1982, is still the Lobos' single-game scoring record.

After being dormant for four seasons (1987–1991), former University of Utah standout Maureen Eckroth was hired as the head coach for the program as it returned in the 1991–1992 season. Even the program's most fervent fans may have forgotten the names of some of Eckroth's top players: Heidi Harris, Becky Bissell, Amy Clark, and Christy Romero, whose names are still in the program's record book.

Eckroth didn't have much success despite the fact that she was building a program. The Lobos, competing in the WAC, won only 14 games—and just 6 WAC games—in her four seasons. Something else sticking in the craw of her few fans: the Lobos were winless in nine games against New Mexico State during her four seasons. Along the way, UNM lost games by the lopsided scores of 108–45, 100–46, 83–42, 92–22, 95–48, 104–50, and 86–34.

Wins and fans were scarce. It was time to make a change, but where should the Lobos turn?

Enter Don Flanagan, a local basketball legend who had led Eldorado High School to 11 state championships at its helm, taking the Eagles to 401 victories—and losing just 13 times—in 16 seasons. But there's more: 14 tournament championships; 15 district championships; winning streaks of 77, 74, 69, 66, and 60 games; teams averaging 25 wins a year; and nine undefeated seasons.

He turned the Lobos program into a basketball powerhouse, one not only respected throughout the Southwest but all but worshipped by its growing legion of fans. It didn't take long for Flanagan to show he was well prepared to take the reins of a college program: in his first season, he led the Lobos to 14 victories—as many as they'd had in their previous four seasons combined.

To him, playing games in the Pit was a must.

Abby Garchek was a four-year letter winner from 1994–1998, and she still ranks second in career scoring with 1,836 points, averaging 15.8 points per game and leading UNM in scoring for three seasons. She is one of only 13 Lobos with 1,000 career points and 500 career rebounds, and she ranks 10th in career rebounding, 9th in career assists, and 3rd in career steals. Garchek was a member of UNM's first WAC Tournament Championship team and first NCAA Tournament team. Courtesy UNM Athletics.

"We're not playing them at Johnson; I don't even know why they thought about it," Flanagan recalled. "It looks really bad when you only have a few hundred or a thousand fans and you've got a facility that seats 18,000. I said we're going to change that; we're going to get a lot of fan support."

And they did.

"The Pit was always the epitome of playing an important game," he said. "That probably was as important as anything for our success. And then you add some local kids—Katie Kern, Miranda Sanchez, Nikki Heckroth, Judy Vogt, and Lindsey Arndt, to name a few."

Kern had played for Flanagan at Eldorado; the other four hailed from nearby Sandia High School, which had enjoyed success under a man who became Flanagan's assistant at UNM, Ed Wyant. "A lot of them were good kids that were quality kids that weren't on the front page ever—didn't have any problem with discipline," Flanagan said. "You had kids that women and young girls could look up to. It was a solid program."

Fans started turning out to see the Lady Lobos, and the team started turning out wins, thanks to Flanagan's emphasis on fundamentals. One sports writer who covered the Lobos and was in the Pit for Flanagan's early practices noticed that he started with the most basic of fundamentals—almost as if none of his girls had played the game before.

It paid off.

Flanagan said there were several factors in turning a lackluster program into a national brand: he made sure his team would play its home games in the Pit; he recruited good local talent; he made his players get back to the fundamentals; the Lobos started to win games (which attracted more fans); the team didn't shy away from playing anybody; and the team soon became a regular in the postseason.

"We had some great wins there in the Pit; we actually had some great wins at Texas, where

The 1996–1997 Lobo women's team. Courtesy Gary Herron.

An autographed 1997–1998 UNM women's team photo. Coach Don Flanagan said postgame autographs became a distraction, and he had to restrict his players from signing for fans because they were so accommodating. Courtesy Gary Herron.

The Lady Lobos donned hard hats to "celebrate" the start of the $60 million renovation project that took place beginning in 2009. Courtesy J. B. Gallegos.

we beat them twice," Flanagan recalled. "We had beaten—throughout my years—Oklahoma, USC, UCLA, Arizona State, Arizona, Washington—we've beaten almost everybody in the Pac-12. The one we couldn't beat was Stanford and I didn't want to play them again."

In his dozen years at the helm, Flanagan led UNM to 11 straight winning seasons, which included 10 consecutive postseason appearances. During a 12-year span (1997–1998 to 2008–2009), the Lobos had 11 seasons with at least 20 wins.

Just as the men had benefitted from enthusiastic crowds in the Pit, so did the ladies, to the tune of 17 home wins in the 1998–1999 season, part of what became a 24-game home-court winning streak. That impressive streak ended with a loss to Drake in

the quarterfinals of the Women's National Invitation Tournament (WNIT).

In 2001–2002, UNM had gone 22–9 and made the NCAA Tournament for just the second time in program history, and the victories just kept coming.

In arguably his best season (2002–2003), UNM finished with an overall record of 24–9, winning the MWC Tournament and advancing to the Sweet 16 of the NCAA Tournament for the first time in program history.

Flanagan was named MWC Coach of the Year in 2004–2005 and the Russell Athletic/Women's Basketball Coaches Association Region Seven Coach of the Year the following season.

The Lobos in 2007–2008 had extended their NCAA Tournament streak to seven consecutive

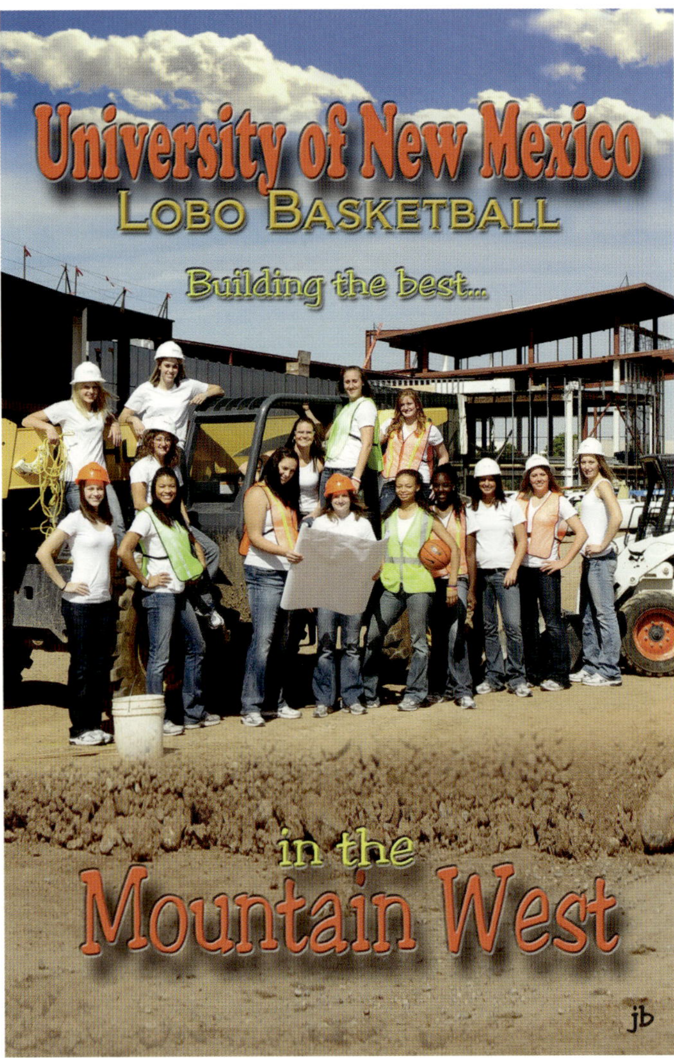

The renovation photo taken by longtime Albuquerque photographer J. B. Gallegos was later used on a poster that carried the title "Building the Best in the Mountain West." Courtesy J. B. Gallegos.

"

We have to play better at home. We seem timid and afraid to make mistakes at home but we need to get over that. We have to win at home.

—Former coach Don Flanagan

seasons and kept "packing the Pit" to enjoy their team's success. The season ended, though, with a heartbreaking 61–60 loss to West Virginia at the Pit.

The 2008–2009 Lobos won 25 games, the second-most wins in school history, extending the impressive postseason streak to 12. UNM won its first three games in the WNIT, 72–44 over Southern in the Pit, then 54–43 over Nebraska, and 61–56 over Oregon State, games played at Rio Rancho's Santa Ana Star Center because of the renovations taking place at the Pit. The fourth time at the Star Center wasn't a charm; UNM lost to Kansas 78–69.

The 2009–2010 team went 19–13, making the postseason for the 13th time. After a 66–51 victory over Southern in the Pit in a WNIT contest, UNM was whipped by Oregon, 93–67, in Eugene. It was Flanagan's final postseason game with UNM.

The Lobos' 2010–2011 slate included Oklahoma, an NCAA Final Four Team in 2010, and the Cal Bears, who won the WNIT. 12 teams on the schedule were coming off postseason play, six of them in the MWC. The aggressive schedule also included Texas Tech; University of California, Irvine; New Mexico State; UTEP; and Arizona.

By the season's end, UNM was 7–7 in conference play and 13–18 for the season—the first losing season in 15 years, which also ended a 13-year streak of postseason play. It didn't help losing 9 of 10 games from December 4 to January 22.

"It was a season in which we spent too much time searching for ways to be successful, and it took us a while to figure that out," Flanagan said at the time. "I still think we should have done better."

Still, loyal Pit fans showed up at an average of 7,677 per game, good for the sixth-ranked spot in the nation—and UNM's best gate since the 2007-2008 season.

Flanagan, the most successful coach in the program's history, officially announced his resignation on April 4, 2011, reading his notes off a

We have such a special opportunity at the University of New Mexico because the whole state is behind us and behind us no matter where we play. . . . To have that many fans there creating that kind of atmosphere was unbelievable. It just shows the pride our fans take in Lobo basketball and it reminds us how much we give back to them.

—Amy Beggin

Guard Nikki Nelson taps her head to signal a play during the 2009–2010 season. Injuries cut short what could have been several good seasons for the girl from Chewelah, Washington. Courtesy J. B. Gallegos.

UNM coach Don Flanagan didn't make a scene on the court—he received very few technical-foul calls in his stint—but here he seems concerned about a referee's call. Courtesy J. B. Gallegos.

folded yellow piece of paper. He thanked the players he had coached during his 16 seasons at UNM, told of his appreciation for the fans, and thanked the university for allowing him to coach the Lobos as long as he did.

Athletic Director Paul Krebs said Flanagan's success at UNM had been "staggering." Flanagan put New Mexico on the map when it came to women's basketball, he said.

Flanagan, inducted into the New Mexico Sports Hall of Fame in 1997, finished with a 340–168 record at UNM, which included just two losing seasons, one of them being that frustrating final season.

"The hiring of Don Flanagan to be the head women's basketball coach at UNM was an incredible hire," Krebs said when the 67-year-old Flanagan announced his decision. "Because of his efforts, the efforts of his staff and his student athletes, in my

A team photo of sorts during the Lady Lobos' 2010 game against MWC foe Air Force. Appearing are (left to right) Nikki Nelson (number 12), Georonika Jackson, Jourdan Erskine (number 14), Porche Torrance (number 23), and Jessica Kielpinski (number 52). Courtesy J. B. Gallegos.

opinion this is one of the most desirable women's [coaching] jobs in the country."

Aside from the glory on the court, his Lobos enjoyed success inside the classroom: in his 16 years, the women's basketball team averaged a 3.22 grade-point average; 102 of his players earned academic all-conference awards; two players made it to the WNBA; and one—Fatima Maddox, who played for UNM in 2003–2004 before transferring to Temple— even played for the Harlem Globetrotters, the ninth female in the team's storied history. (Her nickname with the 'Trotters was TNT.)

Noted for stifling defense under Flanagan, UNM finished among the conference leaders in scoring defense every year and consistently ranked in the top-20 in the nation in that category.

Fan support was tremendous as a result of the Lobos' defense and intense style of play, with the Lobos ranking in the top 5 in the nation in home attendance 7 times in one 11-season stretch, with 13 straight seasons among the top 10.

"Don Flanagan is synonymous with Lobo women's basketball, and his career is unprecedented. Don turned this program around, and not only made the Lobos contenders, but he impacted the lives of so many young women," Paul Krebs said. "What he was able to do with his team on the court and in the classroom from the championships to the academic awards is to be commended. He will be missed."

Oddly, it may seem, Flanagan recently said, "I always thought I was a better high school coach because there I could start them and teach them

Top: The players were always accommodating to the fans, to the extent of slapping the hands of youngsters as they ran down the ramp before a game. Courtesy J. B. Gallegos.

Bottom: Although this UNM women's game wasn't a sellout, fans flocked to the Pit and did fill it for a number of "Pack the Pit" promotions through the years, and UNM always led the MWC in attendance, ranking 11th in the nation in 2015–2016. Courtesy UNM Athletics.

from the very basics of the game and develop the game, but when you get to the college game, you don't get those kinds of kids. They have different kinds of shots; a lot of times they don't understand—they've been the stars and they got to shoot all the time—and they don't understand the team concept."

Yvonne Sanchez, who had played for him at Eldorado and had later been his assistant at UNM, was named his successor on April 22, 2011, becoming the fifth head coach in UNM women's basketball history. She didn't enjoy the same success her mentor had enjoyed. In fact, she lost a handful of freshmen who departed when Flanagan bid adieu.

As if that wasn't detrimental enough, the 2011–2012 team had to overcome a multitude of injuries before finally making MWC Tournament history, becoming the first seventh seed to beat a second-seeded team at the conference tournament, with an upset win over Boise State pushing the Lobos into the MWC championship game. They were unable to

Sara Halasz (2008–2014) came to UNM from Lakes High School in Lakewood, Washington. By the time her Lobo career ended, she was a 1,000-point scorer. Courtesy UNM Athletics.

A trio of Lobos highlighted this 2015–2016 magnetized schedule, which fans could affix to their refrigerators, keeping them aware of when their favorite team played. Courtesy Gary Herron.

pull off a victory in the finals, but it didn't diminish what they had done.

The 2012–2013 Lobos extended their winning tradition by winning six more games than they won in the previous season and by winning at least one game in the conference tournament for the seventh year in a row.

The 2013–2014 season was forgettable; again beset with injuries, the team limped to a record of 11–19, with a 3–12 mark in games decided by eight or fewer points.

A 1–7 start in 2014–2015 had fans wondering what had become of their beloved team, with some fans calling for Sanchez's firing. Not to worry: Sanchez led the Lobos to victory in 20 of their final 26 games, including a school-record 14 conference wins, to end up with a respectable record of 21–13, with a school-record 14 conference wins and a 13-game winning streak in the Pit. She took the Lobos as far as the MWC tournament championship game. For that, she was named MWC Coach of the Year.

What a difference a season makes.

After completing her fifth season (2015–2016) as the head coach at UNM, this time with a 17–15 (9–9 in the MWC, tied for fifth) record and a 75–67 loss to Weber State in the first round of the Women's Basketball Invitational in Johnson Gym (the Pit was unavailable because of the Ty Murray Invitational), Sanchez was dismissed on March 18, 2016.

"This decision was made after a lot of careful consideration and a variety of factors. We appreciate what Yvonne has brought to our basketball program over her time at New Mexico," Paul Krebs said. "I believe with our facilities, our fan base, and with our commitment to supporting women's basketball, I'm confident that we can hire a coach that can return us to a championship level."

The Lobos had been picked to finish second in the 11-team MWC by the media, for whatever that's worth, and were relegated to fifth place by season's end.

Sanchez ended her UNM career with a record of 77–81 overall and 40–44 in the MWC. Although

> **I remember when we came down The Pit ramp onto the court. There were more than 18,000 people there and most of them were from Gallup. When we walked out after winning, everybody started screaming and it was so uplifting. The amount of people was amazing.**
>
> **—Valerie Kast, former Lobo from Gallup HS)**

the Lobos finished as high as second place in 2014–2015, that was UNM's only winning mark in five MWC seasons. The Lobos were swept by New Mexico State in Sanchez's final season, which also saw an impressive 16-game home-court winning streak come to an end with a 78–69 loss to Duquesne on November 28, 2015.

On March 30, 2016, Krebs announced he had found Sanchez's successor: Mike Bradbury. The head coach at Wright State University for the previous six seasons was given a five-year contract.

Bradbury brought with him to Albuquerque nine successful years as a Division I head coach, the past six with Wright State University in Dayton, Ohio. With the Raiders, Bradbury led his squad to five 20-win seasons, including each of the last

three seasons. In the last three seasons, Wright State amassed a 75–28 record—the best among the 13 Division I programs in Ohio.

"I am excited to have Mike Bradbury lead our women's basketball program," Krebs said in late March. "We looked at a lot of candidates, and Mike rose to the top with his past successes, both as a head coach at Wright State and Morehead State and as an assistant. Mike has a great reputation as a recruiter, as a coach and as an educator."

Top: First-year UNM women's coach Mike Bradbury was selected to replace ousted coach Yvonne Sanchez following the 2015–2016 season. Courtesy J. B. Gallegos.

Bottom: Mike Bradbury apparently wasn't afraid to show excitement as his new team was about to start its season. Courtesy J. B. Gallegos.

"

To come here and play against a team that we respect, and to be in this type of environment is what playing basketball is all about. . . . These fans are knowledgeable and they're gracious."

—Loyola Marymount head coach Julie Wilhoit

One reason for the revitalized interest in women's basketball, including the turnout in the Pit for home games, was because the team's games were being aired on local radio.

For 10 seasons, starting in 2002, Joe Behrend described home and away games for those tuning in to 610-AM, the Sports Animal.

Here are a few of his thoughts from his time courtside.

"I think the energy of the Pit and what Don Flanagan accomplished is one of the greatest success stories in collegiate women's basketball in the country. If you go back 40, 50 years from now, they'll still be looking back at what he accomplished and what the fans accomplished here."

Flanagan, Behrend said, was "very composed—a class act."

He went on, saying, "I think when you look at the women's collegiate game, you'd have to look at his record and put him right up there (with Vivian Stringer and Geno Auriemma) . . . you still look back at his high school record of 401–14 over 16 years and say, 'Is that a misprint?' Incredible."

Most memorable for Behrend, he said, were "all the winning streaks in the Pit; the UNLV sellout; Pack the Pit in '04, '05, and '06—one of a handful of sellouts, 18,000 fans."

From his years at the mic, who would he take to start an all-time UNM team?

"Dionne Marsh, Mandi Moore, Lindsey Arndt, Abby Letz—she was just extremely tough—and Katie Montgomery, Jordan Adams, and Chelsea Grear," Behrend replied, not needing a long time to come up with some of the greats he'd seen in his decade.

That'd be a tough team to beat, with a short but decent bench, thought Behrend.

His favorite Lobo to interview? "Mandi Moore, because she hated to lose and she was always honest."

He wishes the women's basketball team had a comparable reception beyond the Pit.

"It's like night and day for covering New Mexico's women here vs. the Lobos on the road—such a stark contrast," he said. "When you go on the road, you go to BYU, which had a good team, and you might find 40-50 people in the stands. Where is everybody?"

He continued, "Don Flanagan and the whole city really built something here that was unique and really special at that time and I think a lot of teams have tried to duplicate it over the years without the success that we saw here."

Joe Behrend, who began calling women's games in 2002, teamed with former Cibola High and Texas Tech cager Hazel Tull Leach for several seasons on the 610–AM airwaves, then had former UNM standout Nikki Heckroth-Lobato add color to his calls. Courtesy Joe Behrend.

Ken Sickenger of the *Albuquerque Journal* saw many of the games Joe Behrend described on-air, and he fondly recalled some of his personal highlights there.

"UNM women's basketball fans haven't always been satisfied with the win total during my 10 seasons covering the team (2006–2016), but they've certainly enjoyed plenty of exciting moments at the Pit," Sickenger said.

"Nail-biters? There have been many, including several battles between UNM and some of the top women's programs in the country," he said. "We'll get to some of those later, but let's start with a few eye-popping individual performances that brought Pit fans to their feet."

"Several of them came courtesy of Dionne Marsh, including a night to remember on March 8, 2008. Marsh, an undersized but superbly athletic 6-foot-1 post, went into that game against Colorado State needing 11 points to surpass Abby Garchek as New Mexico's career scoring leader. She scored 26 in front of an electric Senior Night crowd of 10,171. Marsh went on to amass 1,913 points but would have loved to score at least two more at the Pit," Sickenger added. "Her final game there was an NCAA Tournament first-round thriller against West Virginia on March 22, 2008. Marsh had a chance to win the back-and-forth battle when she grabbed an offensive board but came up short on a put-back attempt at the buzzer. West Virginia escaped with a 61–60 win that sent more than 12,000 Pit fans home disappointed."

Overall, he said, "The UNM women's basketball program has been on something of a roller-coaster ride in recent years, but Pit fans have remained loyal and been treated to a number of dramatic games.

"They've celebrated dramatic victories, including Amy Beggin's driving layup with 2.5 seconds remaining to edge DePaul on November 17, 2008. They've also suffered heartbreaking losses, including a 70–65 loss to fifth-ranked Stanford on November 24, 2014, in which Clovis native and fan favorite Antiesha Brown missed two free throws with the Lobos trailing by one point lead and 20 seconds remaining."

"Lobos fans have always had a special appreciation for overachievers like the 5-foot-6 Beggin, native New Mexicans like the 5-10 Brown, or players like 2016 grad Alexa Chavez, who fit both categories," he said. "Chavez, a 6-foot Santa Fe native who came to UNM as a freshman walk-on, earned a scholarship with her hard-nosed play and never failed to receive loud ovations from the Pit faithful."

At press time, "Sick" was anticipating the new regime, in light of Sanchez's dismissal. She was added to her brother's staff at Eldorado High School as an assistant coach for Roy Sanchez's boys basketball program.

"A new era of Lobo women's basketball begins in 2016–17 with head coach Mike Bradbury taking over the program," Sickenger said. "But New Mexico retains one of the nation's best and most vocal fan bases at The Pit, where women's basketball games are anticipated events and rowdy fans are part of the attraction."

The $60 Million Renovation

As the twenty-first century approached—remember the Y2K scare as the year 2000 approached?—the departure of Dave Bliss after 10 seasons meant a new coach had to be found. And, by the time this book was being written in 2016, the Lobos had four more coaches, along with a $60 million renovation project to give the Pit a new look.

Fran Fraschilla (1999–2002; 55–41)

The Lobos wanted a proven coach after Dave Bliss said good-bye, and they turned to Fraschilla.

Before arriving at UNM, Fraschilla had been the head coach at St. John's University from 1996–1998, leading the Red Storm to the NCAA tournament in his final season; he had been the head coach from 1992–1996 at Manhattan College; and, before becoming a head coach, Fraschilla worked as an assistant basketball coach for Providence College, Ohio State University, Ohio University, University of Rhode Island, and New York Tech.

"Fran" had been out of coaching for a year, but he was eager to get going in the Pit.

Coach Fran Fraschilla's first team, the 1999–2000 squad that finished 18-14 after a 72-65 loss to Wake Forest in an NIT game in Winston-Salem, North Carolina. Courtesy Gary Herron.

His inaugural campaign at UNM, the 1999–2000 season, marked the debut of the MWC; UNM lost to Utah in the WAC championship game in the 1998–1999 season. The Lobos, Utes, Air Force, BYU, Colorado State, San Diego State, and UNLV made up the new eight-team conference.

UNM had four starters returning—Kenny Thomas was gone, drafted in the NBA draft by the 76ers—and three of them (Lamont Long, John Robinson II, and Kevin Henry) averaged in double figures.

Fran got a reprieve of sorts in his first season, in which UNM went 18-14 overall and 9-5 in the new conference; the postseason included a 64-58 victory over South Florida in the Pit before a 72-65 loss to Wake Forest in Winston-Salem, North Carolina.

In his second of three seasons, Fraschilla guided the Lobos to the MWC championship game, where they suffered a 69-65 loss to BYU, and to the third round of the NIT (in 2001). UNM beat Baylor and Pepperdine at home before an 81-63 loss to Memphis in Memphis.

But the glamour of that MWC championship season began wearing off in the third year of the Fraschilla Regime. There were some questionable activities taking place within the program that were reminiscent of the Lobogate Era.

Star recruit Marlon Parmer, a starting point guard, citing verbal abuse heaped on him by his coach, quit the team in the 2001–2002 season; he was the ninth player to leave the team since Fraschilla arrived. Seven-footer Moustapha Diagne,

Top: The Pit played host to the NCAA's 2000 West Regional, in which Wisconsin beat LSU 61–48 and Purdue beat Gonzaga 75–66, followed by a 64–60 victory by Wisconsin over its Big-10 foe Purdue to advance to the next round. Courtesy Gary Herron.

Bottom: Coach Fran Fraschilla (left) and former coach Bob King flank Mike Roberts, honored before the February 17, 2001, game with San Diego State. Roberts was feted for 35 years of broadcasting Lobo sports. Courtesy UNM Athletics.

from Dakar, Senegal—initially expected to be an important asset to the offense—hardly played for the Lobos because of a degenerative bone condition.

But, as they say, when one door closes, another opens—and so it was for Ruben Douglas, a 6′ 4″ guard who flourished in Parmer's absence. Douglas had been one of the most prolific high school scorers in California; he had initially headed to the University of Arizona in 1998 before transferring to UNM. He went on to lead the nation in scoring with a 28-points-per-game average during the 2002–2003 season as a senior, and he was also named the MWC's MVP (but by then Fraschilla was gone).

The team's image further suffered when it was discovered that it had recorded the lowest grade-point average of any sports program at the university, a cumulative team average of 2.17, barely better than a C.

The *Albuquerque Journal* suggested in an editorial that Fraschilla had lost control of the team and that it was time for UNM to "acknowledge that things are terribly wrong in the men's basketball program. And getting worse."

"It is what it is," Fraschilla told the *New York Times*, in response to the editorial. "[Unfortunately,] Lobo basketball is probably more important to the community than the educational system." (Passionate about more than just hoops, Fraschilla received the National Association of Basketball Coaches Literacy Pioneer Award for his work with the "Dream to Read" program in 2000.)

Rudy Davalos, New Mexico's athletic director, merely said, "All coaches get reviewed at the end of the year. . . . We've had distractions—all teams have."

Fraschilla said he wanted to stay. "I love being here," he said. "I like coaching the Lobos. You have to be thick-skinned, tough-minded. I think being a New Yorker probably has trained me for this."

But on March 17, 2002, citing expectations that were hard to meet, Fraschilla resigned.

His team had barely eclipsed the .500 mark (16–14) and had been blown out by Minnesota, 96–62, in a first-round game of the NIT. He had accumulated a record of 55–41 and gone 21–21 in MWC games, which didn't sit well with Lobos fans or Davalos. He admitted the team had been through a lot of adversity and was looked at by its fans as the city's "pro franchise."

Fraschilla is still in love with college basketball: he joined ESPN as a college basketball game and studio analyst in 2003 and serves as an analyst primarily on Big 12 men's basketball games, is a regular on ESPN's coverage of the NIT, and is a regular on ESPN and ESPNU studio shows.

Ritchie McKay (2002–2007; 82–69)

Prior to his stop in the Duke City, McKay had two-year stints each at Portland State (1997–1998), Colorado State (CSU; 1999–2000) and Oregon State (2001–2002). With CSU, a longtime foe of the Lobos, McKay posted a 37–23 record, which included a 1999 NIT berth.

The losing started early: sophomore Patrick Dennehy, a 6' 9" post recruited by Fran Fraschilla, walked out of McKay's first practice session in April! He'd led the Lobos in rebounding the season before. And Marlon Parmer, dismissed by Fraschilla, was not allowed to rejoin the team, despite the coaching change.

McKay's first year (2002–2003) marked the Lobos' third straight conference losing season, but senior guard Ruben Douglas, the MWC's Player of the Year, was a bright spot. It was Douglas's final season at UNM, as he finished his brief 86-game career with 1,782 points—fifth all-time at UNM.

I'll never forget against, I believe it was against BYU, and I threw a pass to Danny, who sealed Rafael Araujo, right to Danny's hand and he laid it in to win the game.

—Troy DeVries (2003–2005); January 26, 2004; UNM 65, BYU 63

Coach Ritchie McKay signals a play from the sidelines during his time in the Pit. Courtesy UNM Athletics.

Mike Roberts (left) and color commentator Joe O'Neill during a game in the Pit. Courtesy Gary Herron.

The program for the 2002 NCAA first- and second-round games played in the Pit. Arizona and Missouri moved on to the next round. Courtesy Gary Herron.

"

I'll never forget when we beat Utah, when they were ranked 10 or 11 in the country and had Andrew Bogut as the number one pick, and we beat 'em here in the Pit—and the fans rushed the court.

—Danny Granger (2003–2005);
February 21, 2005;
UNM 65, Utah 54

The Lobos failed to win a road game that season, and UNM saw its road losing streak grow to 17 in a row—the longest skid since it lost 37 in a row between 1956–1957 and 1959–1960.

The season was marred by a serious, career-ending injury to senior guard Senque Carey, who suffered a spinal cord injury in a November 25, 2002, game against Northwestern State while trying to take a charge. Carey had surgery on January 27, 2003, to remove a bulging disc and fuse vertebrae in his neck; that surgery was performed at Stanford Medical Center in Palo Alto, California.

In all, Carey had played 30 games in 2001–2002, after transferring to UNM from the University of Washington. He started 20 of those games, averaging 6.0 points and 4.1 rebounds per game, and was the team leader in assists, with 95.

Without Carey, the Lobos had just 10 players, including 4 walk-ons; the 8 scholarship players had combined for just eight years of NCAA Division I experience, three of those by Douglas.

Two-year UNM standout Danny Granger stayed involved with basketball in New Mexico. He is seen here during a youth camp in the Davalos Center, and he also lent his name and financial contributions to the Danny Granger Ambassadors club team. Courtesy Gary Herron.

That wasn't all: Sophomore Michael McCowan left the team on February 26, leaving UNM with just nine players, which included two walk-ons. Two more departed after the season—sophomores Jamaal Williams and Chad Bell—leaving McKay with only six returning lettermen and four starters for the 2003–2004 season.

But out of the depths . . .

McKay's tenure was highlighted by an MWC championship in 2005, which earned the Lobos their first NCAA Tournament appearance in six years—and the program's first conference title since 1996. They'd been picked to finish fourth, and with the 26 wins they got to the NCAA Tournament for only the third time in school history.

In the 2005–2006 season, Mark Walters earned first-team all-conference honors under McKay's guidance, marking the first time in MWC history that an institution had a first-team honoree for five straight years. Before Walters, who was a graduate of Highland High School in Albuquerque, McKay had taken a virtual unknown in Danny Granger and turned him into a third-team All-American and an MVP of the conference tournament in 2005, with the Indiana Pacers selecting him as the 17th overall pick in the 2005 NBA draft.

The 2004–2005 campaign was highlighted by 26 victories, the second-highest total in the program's 103-year history.

Of the 13 Lobos who concluded their collegiate eligibility at UNM during McKay's tenure, 8 received their diplomas.

But the Lobos desperately needed to escape the mediocrity of the Ritchie McKay era, as the

2006–2007 season marked only the Lobos' second
losing season in the past 24 years—and highly
regarded Steve Alford needed UNM to escape
the brewing storm in Iowa City.

"I personally liked Ritchie," Krebs said. "I thought
he was a nice man, but we came to the conclusion
that it would be necessary to part ways. The savvy
of this media market, the intensity of the glare of
being a head coach, I thought we were going to
need somebody who could stand up to the press."

So that "somebody" became Steve Alford, whom
Krebs knew wouldn't shy away from big expectations.

The departing McKay's salary of about $550,000
was increased by more than $400,000 to sign
Alford to an initial contract of $975,000.

"People might argue that a near-million dollar
contract is way beyond the average for this state and
for the Mountain West Conference," Krebs wrote in a
letter to the *Albuquerque Journal* on April 13, 2007.
"Our response is we have no intention of being average. We want to compete with the best in the country. This investment in Lobo men's basketball says
we've readied ourselves to play at the highest level."

Postscript: McKay, head coach at Liberty
University, was voted Big South Coach of the Year
following the 2015–2016 season by the league's
head coaches and media. McKay returned to
Liberty before the season began after spending
six seasons as an associate head coach at Virginia.

*Top: Vice President of Athletics Paul Krebs has
come under fire by Lobos fans; he's the guy who
basically decides who to hire and who to fire
and, naturally, not everyone agrees with every
decision. Courtesy UNM Athletics.*

*Bottom: Lobo coach Ritchie McKay speaks to the
media after a game during his tenure as men's head
coach, 2002–2007. Courtesy UNM Athletics.*

- **September 23, 2002:** UNM celebrates its 100th season of basketball by having more than five dozen former players and coaches attend the Lobo Legend Gala at the Pit. In conjunction with that, balloting by more than 2,000 fans revealed the school's all-time coach (Bob King) and team—Michael Cooper, Mel Daniels, Ruben Douglas, Petie Gibson, Ira Harge, Marvin Johnson, Luc Longley, Royce Olney, Charles Smith, and Kenny Thomas.

- **January 26, 2004:** Danny Granger goes in for a buzzer-beating, game-winning lay-up off a half-court pass from Troy DeVries in UNM's 65–63 win over BYU.

- **February 21, 2005:** As 21 scouts watched the every move of future pros Danny Granger and Andrew Bogut, Mark Walters orchestrated the Lobos' offense and played his usual stifling defense, also scoring a game- and season-high 22 points. His first trey gave UNM a 22–19 lead and it never trailed again; later, with the Lobos leading 51–42, he scored the next 7 points, pushing the margin to 14, and the Utes saw their 18-game winning streak end. Strangely, several enthusiastic Lobo fans painted their faces and bodies in an effort to show support, later rushing the court after the game to celebrate with their Lobo heroes. The combination of body art and sweat resulted in permanent stains to the white uniforms. Still waiting for new gear, UNM had to wear its red road uniforms in the final home game against CSU (UNM 65, CSU 54).

- **November 19, 2005:** The Lobos drub Mississippi (Ole Miss) by 53 points, which ties the record for the fifth-widest point margin in the Pit (UNM 95, Ole Miss 42).

- **March 1, 2006:** The Lobos hold UNLV to the Rebels' lowest point total in school history in a 47–39 victory. UNLV shoots a meager 24.2 percent in the setback.

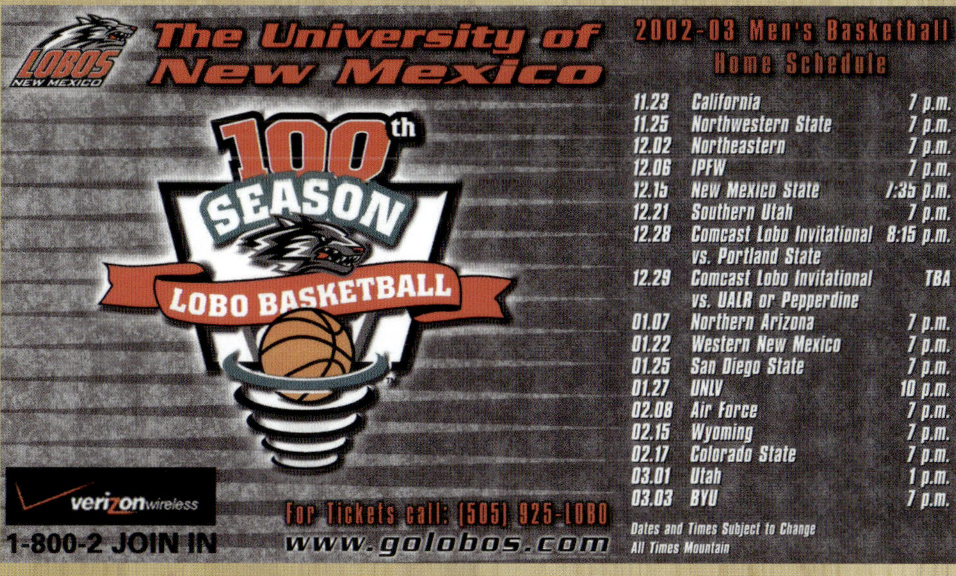

Magnetic UNM men's basketball schedules can be seen on fenders, bumpers, and elsewhere—including refrigerators—throughout the Albuquerque metro area. Courtesy Gary Herron.

Steve Alford (2007–2013; 155–52)

McKay's last team had finished last in the MWC, so there was only one direction for the former Indiana Hoosier star, and Indiana's "Mr. Basketball" in 1983, to go: up.

The Lobos experienced their most successful seasons during Alford's six years at the helm, with three NCAA appearances in a four-year span (2010, 2012, and 2013). The Lobos won or shared the MWC title four times, winning the conference tournament three years in a row (2012–2014); he was named MWC Coach of the Year three times.

The 2009–2010 edition won a school-record 30 games, opening with a 12-game winning streak and, after enduring three losses in a 5-game stretch, assembled another lengthy winning streak—this time, 15 in a row before a loss to San Diego State in the conference tournament. UNM headed to the NCAAs for the first time since the 2004–2005 season but, after a win in the regionals in San Jose over Montana, was whipped by Washington 82–64.

(left to right) Curtis Dennis, Jamal Fenton, and Chad Adams celebrate their team's 2009–2010 regular-season MWC title. Courtesy Tim March for Moji Photography.

"

I'll never forget senior night in 2009. We won in front of 18,018 against Utah with big, old Luke Nevill. That was the last sold-out game with the old seating capacity before the renovations happened to the Pit—a special game for me personally to be a part of.

—Daniel Faris (2005–2009; March 3, 2009;
UNM 77, Utah 71

Top: The northeast corner of the Pit in 2008, before the massive $60 million renovation project. Courtesy J. B. Gallegos.

Middle: Construction underway at the Pit's northeast corner, as seen in June 2008. Courtesy J. B. Gallegos.

Bottom: Rebar lies in the foreground during the massive renovation project, seen here in June 2009. Courtesy J. B. Gallegos.

Top: How the renovation project appeared from across the street, at University Stadium, looking west. Courtesy J. B. Gallegos.

Middle: Looking west, toward the Pit's northeast corner, in 2008. Courtesy J. B. Gallegos.

Bottom: A photo taken in June 2009 from Isotopes Park, showing how the Pit appeared from a distance. Courtesy J. B. Gallegos.

There were some inconveniences for fans during the renovation, namely outdoor toilet facilities, which were used during a 2009 game. Courtesy J. B. Gallegos.

Fans didn't have to endure much, other than being cold at times, during the Pit renovation, as the games went on. Courtesy J. B. Gallegos.

Progress is being made, as seen here looking at a sign near the Pit's northeast corner. Courtesy J. B. Gallegos.

Top: The sparkling "new" Pit, as it appeared on March 28, 2011. Courtesy J. B. Gallegos.

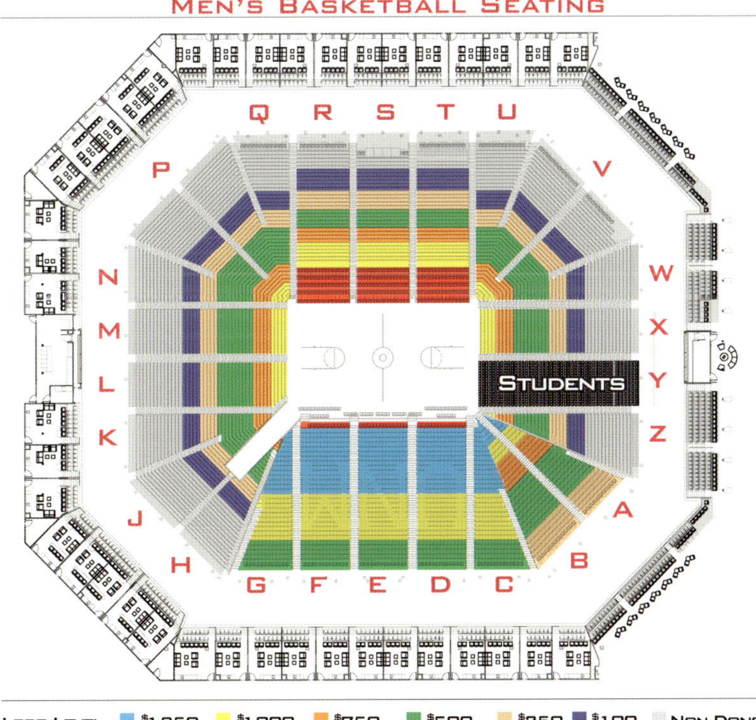

Bottom: Can you find your section? How about your seat? Here's the Pit's seating chart for men's basketball. Courtesy UNM Athletics.

Lobo Level
All sections/rows.....$1,250 per seat

Chairbacks (Sections C-G)
Rows 20-32 ....$1,250 per seat
Rows 10-19 ....$1,000 per seat
Rows 5-9 ....$500 per seat

Chairbacks (Sections A&B)
Rows 30-32 ....$1,250 per seat
Rows 26-29 ....$1,000 per seat
Rows 20-25 ....$750 per seat
Rows 10-19 ....$500 per seat
Rows 5-9 ....$250 per seat

Benches (Sections H-Q & U-Z)
Rows 41-45 ....$1,000 per seat
Rows 36-40 ....$750 per seat
Rows 26-35 ....$500 per seat
Rows 21-25 ....$250 per seat
Rows 16-20 ....$100 per seat
Rows 1-15 ....Non-Donor

Benches (Sections R-T)
Rows 30-36 ....$1,000 per seat
Rows 26-29 ....$750 per seat
Rows 21-25 ....$500 per seat
Rows 16-20 ....$250 per seat
Rows 10-15 ....$100 per seat
Rows 5-9 ....Non-Donor

The 2010–2011 team added UCLA transfer Drew Gordon and hopes were high—maybe not for another 30-win season, but for a return to the Big Dance. It didn't happen, though, as UNM finished 22–13 after a loss to Alabama in the second round of the NIT in Tuscaloosa.

The Lobos won a total of 57 games, including MWC regular-season and tournament titles, in the next two seasons, but they could get no deeper than the second round of the NCAA, beating Long Beach State in the first round in 2012 before a loss to Louisville.

In 2011–2012, UNM went 28–7 and finished 14th nationally in scoring defense and rebound margin, 7th in field goal percentage defense, and 6th in scoring margin. UNM's 16.4 assists per game ranked 10th.

Fans that remembered the NCAA loss to Cal State-Fullerton during the days of Stormin' Norman got flashbacks when the 2012–2013 Lobos got the 3 seed and promptly lost to 14th-ranked Harvard, 68–62.

It spoiled what turned out to be Steve Alford's final season, which until the loss to the Crimson had reeled off 29 victories, 14 of them coming away from the Pit. The Lobos went 4–1 against top-25 teams, beating UConn, Cincinnati, UNLV, and Colorado State. Only one of those wins came in the Pit.

UNM had lost 6′ 9″ Drew Gordon and 6′ 8″ AJ Hardeman from the 2011–2012 team; 7-footer Alex Kirk and 6′ 9″ Cameron Bairstow had big shoes to fill that season. They were unproven: Kirk sat out the 2011–2012 season after back surgery, and Bairstow had been a role player.

Kirk ended the season averaging 12.1 points and 8.1 rebounds; Bairstow added 9.7 points per game and 5.9 boards.

Things were looking good to anyone taking a possible view of the 2013–2014 season.

But then, just one week after calling Pit fans the best fans in the world and agreeing to a 10-year extension, Alford was off to UCLA. He replaced Ben Howland, who'd also suffered an NCAA loss—

The jacket doesn't stay on long for Head Coach Steve Alford, seen here standing in front of his team's bench. At lower right, that's longtime UNM Sports Information Director Greg Remington. Courtesy Gary Herron.

"

I'll never forget when we beat BYU there. It was sold-out; you had Jimmer Fredette coming in and we were ranked eight and nine.

—Dairese Gary (2007–2011);
January 29, 2011;
UNM 86, BYU 77

a second-round loss to Minnesota—and who'd been at UCLA for 10 seasons.

Alford said it was hard to leave, and hard to tell his team he was leaving; of course, his son, Bryce, went with him to play at UCLA. The Bruins made it to the Big Dance his first two seasons, then finished 10th in the PAC-12 in 2015–2016

"I'm proud of my time and the opportunity given at New Mexico," Steve Alford said. "[But] you're talking about the premier basketball program in the country. This is an opportunity that doesn't come around every day."

UCLA Athletic Director Dan Guerrero said his new coach would get a seven-year, $18.2 million contract—$2.6 million a year plus a $200,000 signing bonus—and a buyout paid to UNM.

Alford endorsed his top assistant, Craig Neal, to replace him at UNM.

Ironically, Alford had enticed Los Angeles product Kendall Williams to UNM, away from UCLA, when the Bruins didn't go through with a scholarship offer for him—and Williams earned conference Player of the Year honors.

- **December 15, 2007:** Freshman Dairese Gary scored a career-high 18 points, going 7-of-11 from the floor and hitting all four of his 3-point tries, in an 80–63 victory over Texas Tech. It gave Alford his second win in five tries against Bob Knight, his coach at Indiana. J. R. Giddens and Chad Toppert added 13 points apiece as the Lobos hit 9-of-11 3-pointers, setting a school record with an 81.8 percentage.

- **December 19, 2007:** Alford "over-reacted" to a call that went against his team in the first minute, bringing a crowd of 17,243 to their feet, en route to an impressive 83–69 victory over the visiting Aggies. It was the Lobos' ninth win in as many outings that season in the Pit, and it avenged a 71–62 loss to NMSU in the Pan Am Center 15 days earlier.

- **March 3, 2009:** Senior Tony Danridge scores a career-high 29 points—which he matched four days later—to lead the Lobos to a 77–71 victory over Utah before a sellout crowd of 18,018.

- **January 27, 2010:** Dairese Gary scores 25 points, including 9 in the final 1:30, as the Lobos upset 12th-ranked BYU and end the Cougars' 15-game winning streak (UNM 76, BYU 72).

- **February 18, 2012:** Drew Gordon torched the visiting Rebels for 27 points and 20 rebounds as the Lobos routed 11th-ranked UNLV in a nationally televised game. UNLV managed only 4 field goals and just 18 points in the second half.

Popular guard Dairese Gary, who played for the Lobos from 2007–2011, making 130 starts. Courtesy UNM Athletics.

Craig Neal (2013-2017;
59-38 through 2015-2016 season)

Neal was Alford's longtime assistant—not only at
UNM but also at Alford's previous stop (University
of Iowa, 2004-2007). He ran the team's offense for
Alford, and he was the logical successor when Alford
left to go to UCLA.

"Coach Neal understands what being a Lobo
is all about," said UNM President Robert Frank.
"He impressed me with his vision, dedication and
passion for leading here."

"I'm truly honored to be the head coach at the
University of New Mexico," Neal said at the time.
"Over the past six years my family and I have been
overwhelmed by the support we have received in
this community."

Added Paul Krebs, "Craig was a major part of a
staff that has not only won championships, but graduated student-athletes, raised our academics to
record levels, and poured a tremendous amount of
energy into our community in the form of service
projects."

Neal, like Alford before him, had a talented son
to play for him. Although Eldorado High School
standout Cullen Neal initially committed to play at
St. Mary's, when his dad was named the head coach
he opted to play for a guy fans affectionately called
"Noodles."

Blessed with a handful of Alford recruits—
including future professionals Cameron Bairstow,
Alex Kirk, and Tony Snell—Neal led the Lobos to a
27-7 record and to the NCAA tournament in his first
season, becoming the first rookie coach in school
history to get them into the NCAAs.

*After an outstanding career at Highland High School,
Chad Adams played four seasons (2009–2013) for the
Lobos. Courtesy UNM Athletics.*

*Guard Roman Martinez played four seasons (2006–2010).
He came to UNM from El Paso Montwood High and was
a fan favorite, as seen by this sign and "fat head" poster.
Courtesy UNM Athletics.*

Alex Kirk, a former standout at Los Alamos High School, finishes through with a dunk during his three seasons at UNM. He made himself eligible for the NBA Draft, ultimately signing as a free agent. Courtesy Tim March for Moji Photography.

"

I'll never forget my very first game, versus Detroit, when I scored my first basket and just threw my hands in the air.

—Alex Kirk (2010–2014); November 13, 2010; UNM 63, Detroit Mercy 63

Cameron Bairstow, another favorite of the Pit fans, goes in for a layup. He was a second-round pick of the Chicago Bulls in 2014, and he was traded by the Bulls to the Detroit Pistons following the 2015–2016 NBA season. Courtesy Tim March for Moji Photography.

There have been a lot of emotional Lobos, and popular Lobos, through the Pit's first 50 seasons, but Hugh Greenwood probably would be listed somewhere among the top 10. Courtesy Tim March for Moji Photography.

The 27 victories in 2013–2014 were the most by a first-year Lobos coach, and Neal then led UNM to the MWC Tournament title, making UNM the conference's first team to win three straight MWC tournaments.

All-American Cameron Bairstow, a senior, became UNM's eighth All-American, and one of four Lobos to earn all-conference honors. Bairstow and Kendall Williams were first-team selections, while Alex Kirk was a third-teamer, and Hugh Greenwood was an honorable-mention selection.

But 10th-seeded Stanford opened its NCAA meeting with UNM on a 20–4 run and, although UNM caught the Cardinal at 45 midway through the

Hugh Greenwood, a popular Lobo during his four seasons (2011–2015), who started
every game in his sophomore, junior, and senior seasons, stands in the spotlight.
Courtesy Tim March for Moji Photography.

Hugh Greenwood drives to the hole at the Pit's south end. Courtesy Tim March for Moji Photography.

I'll never forget on February 18, 2012, when the Lobos beat number 11 UNLV 65–45 on CBS-TV. The crowd was going crazy over an hour before the game and never let up.

—Scott Galetti (KKOB-AM radio broadcaster, 2008–2013)

An enthusiastic Lobo crowd in the Pit. Sorry, we can't tell you the significance of the cat! Courtesy Tim March for Moji Photography.

second half, 11 consecutive possessions without scoring doomed UNM to a one-and-done postseason.

In July 2014, Neal signed a new contract, keeping him as head coach until 2020. (Editor's note: Neal was relieved of his duties in April 2017; former NMSU men's coach Paul Weir was named his successor.)

In the 2014–2015 season, Neal became the second-fastest Lobo coach to win 40 games; his 40th win came in just his 53rd game as head coach, one game more than it had taken Norman Ellenberger to accomplish the feat.

This was a special team, it seemed, becoming the last team in the nation to give up 70 points in a game. Greenwood was a third-team All-MWC selection, becoming only the second guard in UNM history to conclude his career with at least 1,000 points and 600 rebounds.

But it wasn't special enough to get into the postseason, after a loss to Air Force in the conference tournament ended UNM's season at 15–16, including a 7–11 record in the MWC.

UNM has had three players find their ways into the NBA during Neal's tenure: Tony Snell was the 20th overall selection (Chicago Bulls) in the 2013

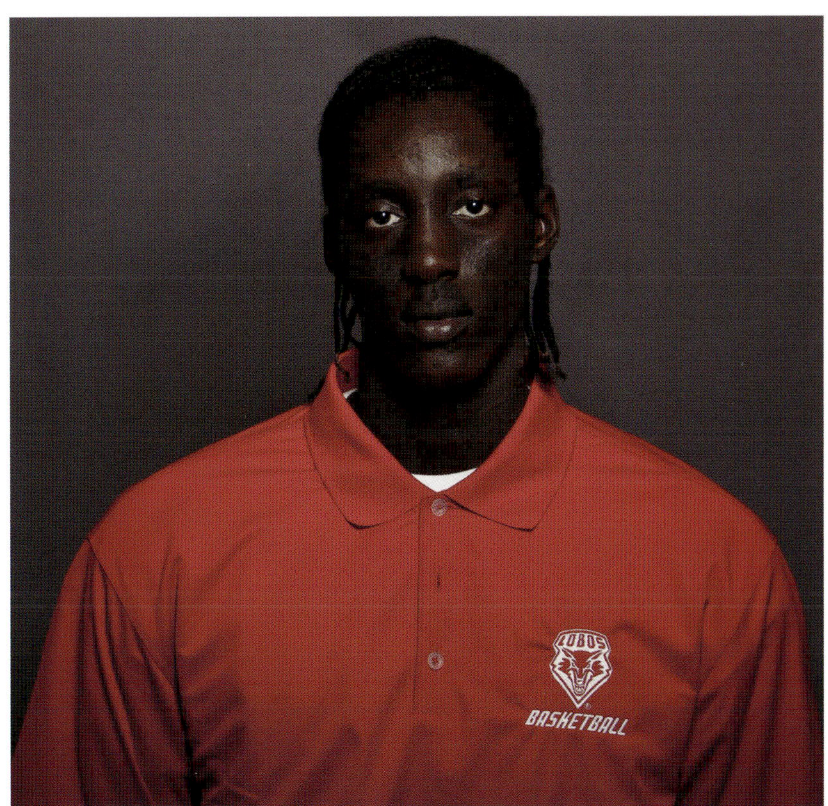

> **"**
>
> **I'll never forget going down the ramp and hearing the Pit fans, seeing how loud they can get, when we enter, and you feel the energy, the excitement.**
>
> —Tony Snell (2010–2013)

I'll never forget when we were playing San Diego State and I remember Kendal Williams finishing a layup on the break and the whole place was so loud it was a dull roar and my ears started ringing.

—Cameron Bairstow (2010–2014); February 27, 2013; UNM 70, SDSU 60

Kendall Williams, a Lobo from 2010 to 2014, goes in for a layup in a game against Air Force. Courtesy Tim March for Moji Photography.

> **I'll never forger it being a wonderful, wonderful place to play at, man. It's like a dream come true—like an NBA arena to me. The whole experience, all the people; the support, the love.**
>
> **—Deshawn Delaney (2013–2015)**

draft, Bairstow joined Snell as the Bulls' second-round pick in 2014, and Alex Kirk landed on the Opening Day roster of the Cleveland Cavaliers in 2014–2015, although he has since gone on to play professionally in Italy. (Snell was traded to the Milwaukee Bucks before the 2016–2017 NBA season began.)

UNM missed the Big Dance in 2015 and 2016, and after the disappointing 2015–2016 season, Cullen Neal decided he was leaving, with a degree in hand and two seasons of eligibility remaining.

Although the fans were outwardly disappointed after the 2015–2016 Lobos lost to Nevada in the first round of the conference tournament and were ultimately denied the chance to get the league's lone NCAA berth (it would go to Fresno State), Neal managed to accomplish something arguably more important in the long run: he has increased the team GPA to 3.15 in the fall semester, breaking a program record his team previously set, and has had five straight semesters of at least a 2.7 team GPA.

Tim Williams launches a free throw during the Lobos' February 27, 2016, game with Fresno State. Courtesy J. B. Gallegos.

Sam Logwood goes in for an uncontested layup in the January 27, 2016, game in the Pit against Air Force. Courtesy Tim March for Moji Photography.

Pit fans always try to shake an opponent at the foul line, unless they're giving grief to an official. Courtesy UNM Athletics.

- **March 7, 2015:** UNM needs overtime to beat Wyoming 52–49 to make it a successful Senior Night, as fans say farewell to Hugh Greenwood and Deshawn Delaney. The victory helped UNM snap what had been an eight-game losing streak.

- **February 17, 2016:** With six minutes remaining, the Lobos trailed visiting Boise State 76–61, then went on an unbelievable 19–2 run to win the game by two points. The comeback was the largest in Lobo history in the final six minutes of a game and the first 15-point comeback since the team's 61–60 win over Texas Tech on Dec. 29, 2010.

The "Voice of the Lobos" in the Pit, as well as at University Stadium for about two decades, Stu Walker passed away from cancer the afternoon of November 2, 2015. The 61-year-old started with UNM in November of 1995, working Lobo basketball during the Dave Bliss era. He was UNM's public address announcer for football when UNM qualified for the Insight.com Bowl in 1997. Courtesy UNM Athletics.

The Death of a Lobo Legend

In a time when it was fashionable for sports fans to discuss who would belong on a Mount Rushmore of, say, baseball's best (yes, Babe Ruth and Ty Cobb for sure, but who else?), or football's best, or hockey's best, and so on, legendary longtime Lobos broadcaster Mike Roberts would arguably be among the quartet of Albuquerque broadcasters.

Although there have been three "Voice of the Lobos" broadcasters over the past 50 years, in the minds of many Roberts will always be remembered as *the* Voice of the Lobos.

After 83 years, countless UNM football and basketball games, and many more countless memories, that staccato voice that so many fans associate with the heyday of Lobo Athletics was silenced. The popular UNM broadcaster from 1966 through 2008 passed away September 13, 2016, at the age of 83 after a battle with cancer.

A gorgeous nighttime photo of the Pit, with a full moon in the distance, all reflected by a recent rainfall. Courtesy J. B. Gallegos.

Starting his career at UNM in 1966 by describing the action at University Stadium, Roberts started calling basketball a year later. Forty-one years after beginning his broadcasting career with UNM, he had the call for UNM's 23–0 victory over Nevada in the New Mexico Bowl in 2007.

It's probably basketball that he is most associated with, because before television deals, it was only the sound of Roberts that would bring Lobo basketball into the living rooms of so many New Mexicans.

Since his death, there has been talk of erecting a statue to Roberts. But where to put it? At University Stadium or at the Pit?

Proud to be a homer for his beloved Lobos, Roberts was known for disagreeing with calls made by officials, and that "homerism" made him a huge hit with most Lobo fans.

His Albuquerque broadcasting career spanned beyond Lobo football and basketball. He was also a longtime play-by-play announcer for the Albuquerque Dukes and the Albuquerque Isotopes, and he even did play-by-play for the short-lived pro volleyball team in the Duke City, the Lasers.

After his UNM career, Roberts called high school games through the 2013 season.

His long broadcast career began in 1951, when he was just 18, in Atmore, Alabama. That was followed by stops in Texas, Florida, Wyoming, and Washington before he became an Albuquerque mainstay.

Talk about being a trouper: many fans remember back in 1992, when just 10 days after undergoing double-bypass heart surgery, Roberts called UNM's 24-7 football victory over Texas Christian University.

Over his distinguished career, Roberts was named New Mexico Broadcaster of the Year 13 times and was inducted into the UNM Athletic Hall of Honor in 1999, where he was named its Distinguished Service Award winner.

Roberts was the 50th inductee and first broadcaster elected to the Albuquerque (now New Mexico) Sports Hall of Fame in 1993, and he was inducted into the Albuquerque Professional Baseball Hall of Fame in 2010.

Former UNM coach Steve Alford solemnly wrote in an email, "Mr. Roberts was simply iconic to all of New Mexico. I'm honored to have known him and worked with him. I always appreciated his kindness and who he was as a person. He loved the Lobos, he loved Albuquerque and he loved New Mexico. All of this passion you could hear, whether it was over the airways or in person."

"The Legend," Mike Roberts (right) ended his career doing high school football and basketball games on the ESPN radio station "The Team" in Albuquerque. Analyst Brian O'Neill (left) was a Lobos assistant coach during Dave Bliss's reign. Courtesy Gary Herron.

Alford was the last UNM basketball coach he worked with. Roberts was fired as the school's play-by-play announcer in April 2008. Governor Bill Richardson declared May 8, 2008, as "Mike Roberts Appreciation Day" throughout the state of New Mexico.

UNM honored Roberts during a 2010 basketball game in the Pit, and he received a loud ovation.

"I've always appreciated them and their support down through the years," he said that evening. "I probably couldn't have lasted as long as I did without them."

Roberts ended every broadcast the same way for his 42 years with UNM: "So long, everybody."

Maybe former Lobo Hunter Greene summed up Roberts's passing the best on social media: "It's a sad day in Lobo Athletics. . . . Mike Roberts, the Voice of the Lobos for over four decades, really gave us all the feeling that we were watching the games live through his accurate play-by-play that he gave Lobo fans. I remember being a freshman and having to help lug his equipment through the airports. Radio was so big back in the day . . . didn't have cable or social media so everyone who was a fan of Lobo basketball tuned in. A huge loss for our community."

Fittingly, and following Bob King and Johnny Tapia, whose bodies had been brought to the Pit floor for viewing and a public good-bye, Mike Roberts was brought to the Pit floor along with some mementos from his years at the microphone, including some recordings of long-ago games. Many in attendance wore red, especially former Lobos.

Mike Roberts, celebrated—and missed—UNM play-by-play broadcaster for countless football and basketball games. Courtesy the University of New Mexico.

"Gathering" More Notoriety

From the first time the Pit was available to have the state high school basketball tournament's finals contested there, it was certainly the place to be.

Although there have been a handful of state tournaments at the Pan American Center in Las Cruces, home of the New Mexico State Aggies, the bulk of the boys' tournaments were at the Pit.

The girls didn't get a state basketball tournament until 1973 and, like the boys, they have been regulars in the Pit, although in 2000 the girls played in the Pit and the boys were in the Pan Am Center. The following March, the format was reversed: boys in the Pit, girls in the Pan Am Center.

New Mexico Sports Hall of Fame member Don Flanagan gets the majority of credit for getting the state high school girls tournament in the Pit.

Before he was the UNM women's head coach, he was the girls basketball head coach at Eldorado High School, a virtual dynasty in the last decade of the twentieth century.

Semifinal, consolation, and championship games in classes AAA and AAAA were played in the Pit for the first time in 1990; quarterfinal and semifinal games in classes A and AA were played in the Pit, with those classes' earlier rounds contested in high

> **I'll never forget the first televised game in the history of the NMAA, the 1971 Class AAAA championship game. Mike Roberts called the game. There were about 12,100 people at the game. I only played six guys. We beat Hobbs 81–80.**
>
> **—Jim Hulsman (Albuquerque High School boys basketball coach, 1968–2004)**

school gyms in Albuquerque. Tingley Coliseum was still in use for some state tournament games in the smaller classes through 1994, but by 1995 the Pit was where the girls decided basketball championships.

Truth be told, it didn't matter where Flanagan's Eagles played: Eldorado won the AAAA championship in Tingley Coliseum in 1989, beating Manzano 40–15, and then claimed the AAAA title the next year, beating Cibola 51–25 in the Pit. Except for the 2001 state tournament, held in the Pan American Center in Las Cruces, the Pit has hosted state championship games for the girls since 1990.

"The first time I got any connection with the Pit was either 1992 or '93, when I went to the New Mexico Activities Association and said it's time for the girls to have the state tournament in the Pit," Flanagan recalled. He continued,

I went with a lawyer; it was 17 men on that NMAA committee, and I talked for about half an hour, and they told me all kinds of reasons why they couldn't have the girls: It wouldn't make enough money, the logistics.

They were giving me all these excuses. And then we did bring up the ACLU. It's time.

There have been times in the past when the annual North-South All-Star high school basketball games were been played in the Pit; recently, the games have been played in metro area gyms. Courtesy Gary Herron.

Volcano Vista head coach Lisa Villareal, right, and her Hawks celebrate their 2016 Cass 6A championship, after they rallied from a 9-point halftime deficit to beat Cibola. Courtesy Vincent Maisano.

Every New Mexico boys' dream: playing in the Pit. Here, Hobbs (in white) beat Cleveland in the 2015 Class 6A championship game. Courtesy Gary Herron.

The Melrose Buffaloes won the Class 2A boys basketball championship game in March 2016. Courtesy Gary Herron.

The second annual T-Mobile Invitational was played December 28–29, 2007, in the Pit and featured eight of the top high school teams in the nation, with four boys' and four girls' teams. Included were the La Cueva High School boys and Gallup High girls from New Mexico. Courtesy Gary Herron.

The thing that got me was when the guys were going to state, they were going to the Pit. When the girls were going to state, they were going to the fairgrounds. . . . That floor [in Tingley Coliseum] was awful.

They said it wasn't available; I already had the guy that managed the Pit and he told me the Pit was available, so I brought him over and he said, "Yes, it's available one week before the boys."

So they still voted 17–0. I was so distraught. I went home and somebody called me and said they passed it. I went, "No way. I just left there—it was 17–0." I don't know how it happened; I don't know how it transpired, but we went to the Pit and played the state tournament there.

And then the girls had 10,000 fans at the state championship game there.

Boys or girls, it doesn't matter: the Pit is *the place* for high school basketball championships to be decided.

Former NMAA Executive Director Gary Tripp remarked,

The New Mexico Activities Association is the governing body that runs all the state championships for 17 high school sports. While running quality championship experiences for all the student athletes, coaches and parents in the state, I believe the basketball championships—and more importantly, the games in the famous Pit—are second to none.

I'll never forget the state championship game in 1994 versus West Mesa, because we won state—the only title I had in high school, and the group of guys was awesome. And then the first game [November 30, 1996] I came back, my sophomore year, they beat us [84–77]—it was a close game. Just being on the Pit floor as an opposing player was a lot of fun. Everyone booed me every time I got the ball—it was more motivation.

—A. J. Bramlett
(former La Cueva High School star;
University of Arizona, 1995–1999)

The stuff dreams are made of: the Rio Rancho Rams were on a five-game losing streak and given the number 11 seed for the Class 6A state tournament in 2016. All the Rams did, after winning a first-round game at Albuquerque High, was roll over Cibola, Cleveland, and Carlsbad in their tournament games in the Pit en route to the championship. Courtesy Gary Herron.

The NMAA state basketball tournament may just be the best high school athletic tournament in this nation. Directors from the National Federation of High School Sports—from Florida, Texas, Nevada and Wyoming—have visited the tournament and the championship games in the Pit and were all nice in saying that this is either the top tournament or is in the top-five in the nation.

It is pretty clear that every single community around this Land of Enchantment flocks to the Pit the second week in March every year to watch their alma mater, son, daughter, grandchild, or whoever have the opportunity to run down the runway of the famous venue and, hopefully, raise the blue trophy at the end of the tournament.

"I have witnessed an 8 a.m. championship game on a Saturday between Mora and Pecos and seen 8,000 tickets sold," Tripp said. He continued,

Many people do not believe me when I tell them this because [the communities of] Mora and Pecos combined today do not have 8,000 residents!

They also love the Pit. It amazes everyone around this great state that Española, Las Cruces, Hobbs, Clovis, Santa Fe, Farmington, etc., can match fan-for-fan all the local area teams from Rio Rancho, Los Lunas, Bernalillo and Albuquerque.

From the perspective of this former director of the NMAA, the state basketball tournament

and the games in the Pit are the strongest bonding event for and by the people of New Mexico. The famous Albuquerque International Balloon Fiesta might be a bigger economic event; however, it brings many people from outside the state and our nation and there is no bonding by all the residents of this state.

We are blessed to have great students, quality parents raising them, excellent coaches as educators, an NMAA that knows how to do things and a little luck, as we are the only ones in this wonderful nation that have the Pit.

Incidentally, although every Lobo men's basketball fan can tell you Marvin "Automatic" Johnson owns the single-game scoring record in the Pit, that's only for the Lobos. Mike Nañez of Melrose High School scored 52 points in his team's 92–83 loss to Grady in the 1995 Class A championship game in the Pit.

"

I'll never forget because of the magnitude of it— my Ralph Tasker story. [My Cougars] were playing Hobbs in a consolation game. We lost to them and I remember so clearly after the game was over there was this massive rush of media to the court. I thought, What's going on? Coach Tasker walked over to me, he was using a cane and brushed the reporters aside, and shook my hand, said you have a good team—your team played well. And as I walked away I realized that was the last game he would coach in his career. . . . It was an honor to be in that situation.

—Brian O'Neill (former Cibola High basketball coach; former Lobo assistant coach); March 14, 1998; Hobbs 88, Cibola 62

"Lighting up" the Pit for a recent Professional Bull Riders' Ty Murray Invitational in the Pit, where it's been held annually since 2009. Courtesy Vincent Maisano.

The Ty Murray Invitational

"This is no B. S. right here; Albuquerque has become a very special stop for a couple reasons," Murray, a native of Peña Blanca, New Mexico, said in a 2016 interview. "Number 1, geographically, [where it's] located, we are able to get the very best bulls every time. Number 2, the fans in New Mexico—Albuquerque, the Navajo Nation and surrounding areas—over the last 18 years of us coming here, have gained a real knowledge of the sport."

"That makes it great and it magnifies the level of electricity you feel in The Pit," he said. "It's not only fun for the fans but it's fun for the riders—a home field advantage. Also, it's an event on tour for 18 straight years—it's almost become an event that's steeped in tradition."

Murray knows the sport has its naysayers, but he thinks once they've witnessed an event up close, they'll change their minds.

"I try to do everything I can," he said. "I feel like it's part of my mission to help the rest of the world see and understand, have a level of appreciation for what our guys do. It's so hard for our people to understand, not only from a physical standpoint, but the mental aspect."

"All sports have winning and losing, hero and embarrassment; our sport has that pressure and

Ben Jones holds on for dear life for eight seconds on a rank bull, en route to the Australian's 2011 victory at the Ty Murray Invitational in the Pit. Courtesy Vincent Maisano.

PBR cowboy Stormy Wing was fortunate to be able to walk away from this "wreck," after he was tossed by Stone Sober at the 2015 Ty Murray Invitational in the Pit. Courtesy Vincent Maisano.

possibility of living or dying," he added. "It's intense—it makes other sports seem not that 'extreme.'"

Although not everyone thought moving the Ty Murray Invite to the Pit in 2009 was a good idea, in retrospect it was. As Murray described,

I think it's been amazing; we wanted to go to the Pit originally. At the time, PBR was new; they were like, what is this? Bull riders and dirt? As PBR started having success and they understood what we are, and we do this in the biggest venues—Madison Square Garden, AT&T Stadium in Dallas—I'm glad they decided to have us as a partner.

I think it's one of the neatest places; you can feel the excitement in the air, and everyone's feeling that energy. It's a fantastic arena for this sport—as far as what the spectators get to experience, and what the athletes get to experience. There's a certain noise level and electricity level. It's small so everyone's on top the action, and there's not a bad seat—everyone's in the eye of the storm.

During the 2016 telecast (on CBS Sports Network), Murray said of his event at the Pit, "This is the Wrigley Field of bull riding—it is like bucking bulls in your grandmother's basement."

A fan's view of the Ty Murray Invitational in the Pit, as seen from the southeast corner, near the ramp, which the bulls come down to get to the floor. Courtesy Vincent Maisano.

NCAA Volleyball

In December 1991, the NCAA Women's Volleyball Championship had first-round matches in the Pit, including the host Lobos versus Washington State University. UNM beat the Cougars 3–1, but then fell in the second round to eventual national champ UCLA, 3–0. UCLA beat Stanford in the West Regional final 3–0 and headed to Pauley Pavilion, where the Bruins beat Long Beach State 3–2 in the national championship match.

In December 1992 the Pit hosted volleyball's Final Four (UNM was eliminated 3–1 by Arizona State in the West Regional's first round).

In the Division I semifinal matches, UCLA won its 43rd match in a row, beating Florida 3–0; Stanford beat Long Beach State 3–1 in the other semifinal.

Then, on December 19 in front of a crowd of 4,693, Stanford stunned first-ranked UCLA 3–1 for its first national volleyball title.

Surprisingly, perhaps, the Bruins had beaten the Cardinals in two previous meetings that season.

In recent seasons the UNM volleyball team had played its high-profile matches in the Pit, including a 2016 showdown with defending national champ Nebraska. That September 10 match, played on the final day of the three-day Lobo Classic, attracted a crowd of 4,473 fans; they saw the first-ranked 'Huskers sweep the Lobos.

ABA, NBA, and WNBA Preseason Games

The Pit has been an attractive venue for preseason ABA and NBA games, dating back to a meeting between Washington and Denver on February 3, 1970, won by Washington 142–125 and attracting 5,611 fans.

In another ABA preseason encounter at the Pit, the Floridians, with former Lobos Ira Harge and Willie Long, and the Denver Rockets met before the 1971–1972 season.

The following NBA preseason games have taken place in the Pit: 1980 (San Antonio vs. Houston); 1992 (Chicago vs. Minnesota); 1996 (Chicago vs. Seattle); 1995 (Utah vs. Golden State); 1997 (Houston vs. Dallas); 1999 (Portland vs. L.A. Lakers, drawing 13,150 fans); 2000 (Sacramento vs. Vancouver); 2001 (Phoenix, with former Lobo Daniel Santiago vs. Houston, with former Lobo Kenny Thomas); 2005 (Sacramento vs. Phoenix); and 2007 (Sacramento, with Kenny Thomas vs. Utah).

On May 5, 2004, former UNM women's standout Abbie Letz and her Minnesota Lynx faced the Sacramento Monarchs in a WNBA preseason game. Two years later, on May 9, the Connecticut Sun met the Sacramento Monarchs

Who better to put on a card, perfect for autographs, for a 2001 NBA exhibition at the Pit than former Lobo standout Kenny Thomas? Courtesy Gary Herron.

in a WNBA preseason contest; and on May 28, 2011, the Los Angeles Sparks faced the Phoenix Mercury in yet another WNBA preseason game.

Harlem Globetrotters

The world-famous basketball team, celebrating its 90th year in "business" with a stop in the Pit in February 2016, has displayed its talents here numerous times.

In their 2012 appearance, the team included a former Lobo women's basketball player: Fatima Maddox, a 5' 6" point guard dubbed "TNT," had played at UNM from 2003–2004 before transferring to Temple.

Concerts

Almost since the Pit opened, concerts have proven to be successful events.

Although officials at the arena said they only had a list dating to September 1993, a post on "Memories of New Mexico" on Facebook revealed countless great acts that have provided entertainment at the Pit, although the exact dates were unavailable. The Pit can hold a maximum of 13,480 for concerts.

The following is an inexact list of acts/performers who have entertained in the Pit over the years, garnered from Facebook respondents: Led Zeppelin; Taylor Swift; Bob Seger; Doobie Brothers; Queen; Mel Tillis; Neil Young; Stone Ponies

Hubert "Geese" Ausbie gives a "goose" to an official during the Harlem Globetrotters 1981 game at the Pit. The 'Trotters seem to visit the Pit to delight audiences almost every other year. Courtesy Gary Herron.

with Linda Ronstadt; Three Dog Night; Nirvana; "Jesus Christ, Superstar"; Dolly Parton and Kenny Rogers; Rolling Stones; Linda Ronstadt; Emerson, Lake & Palmer; War and Tower of Power; Boston; Foreigner; .38 Special and Peter Frampton; Charlie Daniels Band; REO Speedwagon; Billy Joel; Elton John; Jethro Tull; Commodores; Randy Travis and Alan Jackson; and Van Halen.

The Pit's records, dating only to 1993, list the following acts: Elton John; Eagles; George Strait; Pavarotti; Red Hot Chile Peppers; Gaither Home-coming; James Brown; Newsboys and Mariachi Spectacular; George Strait (2009 and again on his "The Cowboy Rides Away Tour" on April 5, 2013, with Martina McBride and the Randy Rogers Band); and Legacy Church (who packed the Pit on December 23, 2015, for two performances of "A Legacy Christmas").

Years before that, evangelist Billy Graham had packed the place.

Boxing Matches

On October 12, 1994, Top Rank presented a boxing card of great interest to Duke City fight fans: Johnny Tapia, Danny Romero, and "Irish" Sean McClain—and all three won their bouts.

Tapia, who scored a TKO over Henry Martinez that day, was 4–0 in his bouts at the Pit, each time with unanimous decisions: February 10, 1995, over Jose Rafael Sosa; February 13, 1998, over Rodolfo Blanco; and January 8, 2000, over Jorge Eliecer Julio.

Fans also remember the late, great Bobby Foster fighting there.

Memorials

With the city and boxing scene in the metro area mourning the death of its homegrown, five-time world champion, Johnny Tapia, the Pit served as a public viewing and memorial service for Tapia on the evening of Sunday, June 3, 2012.

Nearly 7,000 people showed up. Tapia's casket was positioned in the middle of a boxing ring set up in the arena, with boxing gloves and roses adorning the top of the casket, and action photos of him displayed along the sides. Former heavyweight boxer Mike Tyson was a speaker, and video tributes came in from other boxing greats and event promoters around the world.

It was the second memorial service for a local hero; legendary men's basketball coach Bob King had also had his services conducted December 15, 2004, in the Pit.

The third came in September 2016: that was for legendary Lobos broadcaster Mike Roberts, like Bob King a member of the New Mexico Sports Hall of Fame.

Graduations

Albuquerque Public Schools, Rio Rancho Public Schools, and UNM have been holding graduations in the Pit for numerous years, although Rio Rancho has been holding commencement ceremonies for Cleveland and Rio Rancho high schools in recent years at Santa Ana Star Center. Albuquerque Public Schools also made a recent move, to Tingley Coliseum.

UNM still holds its graduations in the Pit.

Tennis

To date, three special tennis events have been held in the Pit, each featuring notable players.

The first was on January 12, 1983, proclaimed "Tennis Day in Albuquerque" by Mayor Harry Kinney.

Thousands of proud parents and family members used to fill the Pit for high school graduations, which have since moved to the fairgrounds. This is Eldorado High School's 1999 commencement exercise. Courtesy Gary Herron.

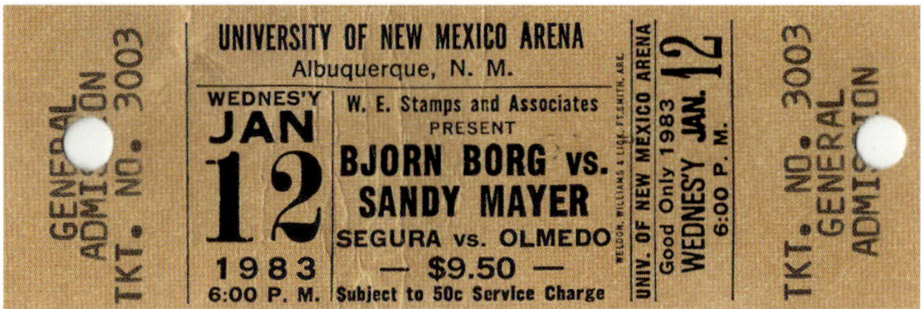

Above: A ticket stub from tennis legend Bjorn Borg's 1983 match against Sandy Mayer. On the "undercard," Pancho Segura faced Alex Olmedo. Courtesy Gary Herron.

Left: Bjorn Borg took time to chat with fans and sign autographs after his exhibition match in the Pit on January 12, 1983. Courtesy Gary Herron.

Alex Olmedo squared off against legendary Pancho Segura in the first match, and then Bjorn Borg, two years since retiring from the pro game, defeated Sandy Mayer, three sets to one. A crowd of more than 6,300 was on hand.

On December 3, 1986, two fan favorites met on the Pit floor. Chris Evert was defeated by Martina Navratilova in that get-together, 7–6, 6–4.

And on September 12, 2008, an estimated 4,000 fans turned out to see Pete Sampras face Sam Querrey in the Pit. Writing his story in the *Albuquerque Journal*, sports writer Toby Smith noted, "With only 12 feet of space behind the baseline of the blue synthetic court placed on the Pit's famed hardwood floor, spectators at both ends of the court spent much of the night jumping out of the way of 120 mph serves blasted by Sampras and Querrey." Sampras, 17 years older than his opponent, won 6–7 (4), 6–3, 6–1.

Gymnastics

There is no better place to fill for top-notch gymnastics than the Pit, which played host to coach Rusty Mitchell's nationally known program when it

US gymnast Kurt Thomas performs on the pommel horse at the 1981 gymnastics exhibition at the Pit. Courtesy Gary Herron.

US gymnasts enter the floor during a 1981 performance at the Pit. Courtesy Gary Herron.

existed (1966–1999) at UNM, and then featured the US men's team in a 1981 exhibition. Mitchell was a member of the 1964 US men's Olympics team.

In 1991 the US men's team beat Romania in a dual meet, and in 1993 the Pit was home to the NCAA men's gymnastics championships.

Gathering of Nations

The world's largest gathering of Native American and indigenous people took place every year at the Pit in late April for more than three decades.

In 2016 the 33rd annual Gathering of Nations, considered the most prominent Native American powwow in the North America, hosted tens of thousands of people and more than 700 tribes from

The poster for what may have been the final Gathering of Nations Powwow in the Pit in 2016. Courtesy James Korenchen and Associates.

Opening ceremonies delight thousand at the Pit in the 2015 Gathering of Nations. Courtesy James Korenchen and Associates.

throughout the United States, Canada, and around the world.

The three-day event included more than 3,000 traditional Native American singers and dancers competing, and more than 800 Native American artisans, craftsmen, and traders displaying and selling their work. In addition, contemporary indigenous music groups performed a wide variety of musical genres on stage.

Vendors in the Native Food Court offered guests a large selection of food choices ranging between southwestern-style cuisine and traditional Native American fare.

Every year, as part of the Gathering of Nations, a young Native American woman is crowned Miss Indian World and represents all native and indigenous people as a cultural goodwill ambassador.

Although the songs, dances, and storytelling have been shared among tribes for thousands of years, powwows have come into the social gathering tradition only recently.

"The Gathering of Nations is the world's largest powwow, bringing people together from throughout the United States and around the world to the event each year," said Derek Mathews, founder of the Gathering of Nations. "The Gathering of Nations strives to be a positive cultural and spiritual experience that is exhilarating for everyone. The powwow features thousands of dancers performing different styles from many regions and tribes, offers the finest in Native American arts and crafts in the Indian Traders Market, a delicious variety of Native American and Southwest cuisine, and the best in contemporary entertainment performances."

The Gathering of Nations opened with the Miss Indian World competition at the Albuquerque Convention Center. It was followed by the much-anticipated "Grand Entry," where thousands of Native American dancers simultaneously entered the arena dressed in colorful outfits to the sounds of hundreds of beating drums; it began at noon on

An elder dancer at the 2015 Gathering of Nations in the Pit. Courtesy James Korenchen and Associates.

"Tiny Tot Dancers" at the 2015 Gathering of Nations in the Pit. Courtesy James Korenchen and Associates.

the first day and was repeated later that evening and twice on Saturday. The new Miss Indian World is traditionally crowned Saturday evening after the Grand Entry.

Native American people are deeply spiritual. Their songs and dances touch upon the spiritual symbolism that is a part of their daily life.

Powwows are a celebration of the life, heritage, language, and culture of the Indians of North America. A powwow is a time for nations to share, celebrate, and perform with their cultural dances and songs, to meet once again with old friends, to renew their bonds, and to meet new friends. It is a sacred, spiritual, and social event that over time has come to mean more each year to the people of the nations. A nation, in reference to American Indians, is all the tribes that belong to one culture, such as the Cherokee or the Sioux. There are many different powwow styles and hundreds of distinct songs, dances, and traditions that identify each nation.

Hence the Gathering of Nations' importance to America's history—and no state boasts more Native Americans than New Mexico.

On May 4, 2016, UNM announced that the Pit would no longer be the host for the event. The event was to be moved to Tingley Coliseum on EXPO New Mexico, the state fairgrounds, for the immediate future.

University Arena—called "the Pit" by the bulk of the population—as it looks today. No matter what you call it, it's a gorgeous venue with entertainment options throughout the year. Courtesy J. B. Gallegos.

Battle of the Rio Grande

Starting in 2015, a fundraising all-Lobos exhibition contest was staged at the Pit, attracting a crowd of about 9,500.

That event, coordinated by former Lobo standout Cameron Bairstow, allowed Bairstow to donate $11,000 of the proceeds to the Lobo Club and $5,000 to the Pink Pack Foundation, started by his former teammate, Hugh Greenwood.

The 2015 event was so popular that on June 25, 2016, the Battle of the Rio Grande drew an estimated 6,000 fans to the Pit to see former UNM stars take on one-time Aggie cagers.

The Lobos beat the Aggies 102–97. UNM had six players scoring in double figures, with the game's MVP, J. R. Giddens, pouring in 20 points, with 7 rebounds and a couple of steals. Former Lobo Troy DeVries had 19 points, Roman Martinez added 11, and Dairese Gary and Alex Kirk chipped in with 10 points apiece.

Former Aggie Jonathan Gibson was the high-scorer with 32 points.

Significant Numbers from a Half Century of Action in the Pit

Lobos in the NBA Draft (first-round picks in bold)

YEAR	PLAYER/POSITION	YEARS AT UNM	NBA TEAM	ROUND/PICK
1956	Toby Roybal/G	1953–1954, 1955–1956	N.Y. Knicks	N/A
1964	Ira Harge/C	1962–1964	Philadelphia 76ers	2nd/11th
1967	Bill Morgan/F	1965–1967	San Francisco Warriors	11th/119th
1967	Ben Monroe/F	1965–1967	L.A. Lakers	12th/127th
1967	**Mel Daniels/F**	**1964–1967**	**Cincinnati Royals**	**1st/9th**
1968	Ron Nelson/G	1966–1968	Baltimore Bullets	3rd/26th
1969	Ron Sanford/F	1967–1969	Cincinnati Royals	4th/51st
1970	**Greg Howard/F**	**1967–1969**	**Phoenix Suns**	**1st/10th**
1970	Ron Becker/F	1967–1970	Baltimore Bullets	10th/168th
1971	Willie Long/C	1968–1971	Cleveland Cavaliers	2nd/35th
1973	Darryl Minniefield/F	1971–1973	Philadelphia 76ers	4th/53rd
1974	Bernard Hardin/F	1972–1974	Portland Trail Blazers	5th/74th
1978	Marvin Johnson/F	1976–1978	Chicago Bulls	2nd/31st
1978	Willie Howard/F	1977–1978	New Orleans Jazz	7th/139th
1978	Michael Cooper/G	1976–1978	L.A. Lakers	3rd/60th
1979	Russell Saunders/G	1977–1979	Kansas City Kings	10th/200th
1979	Phil Abney/F	1977–1979	N.Y. Knicks	6th/113th
1980	Everette Jefferson/G	1978–1980	Houston Rockets	6th/130th
1980	Larry Belin/C	1978–1979	Portland Trail Blazers	5th/102nd
1981	Kenny Page/F	1979–1981	Cleveland Cavaliers	5th/96th
1984	Phil Smith/G	1980–1984	Detroit Pistons	4th/89th
1984	Tim Garrett/F	1982–1984	Washington Bullets	7th/145th
1986	Johnny Brown/F	1984–1986	L.A. Clippers	7th/146th
1987	Kelvin Scarborough/G	1983–1987	Denver Nuggets	6th/123rd
1991	**Luc Longley/C**	**1987–1991**	**Minnesota T'Wolves**	**1st/seventh**
1997	**Charles Smith/G**	**1993–1997**	**Miami Heat**	**1st/26th**
1999	**Kenny Thomas/F**	**1996–1999**	**Houston Rockets**	**1st/22nd**
2005	**Danny Granger/F**	**2003–2005**	**Indiana Pacers**	**1st/17th**
2008	**J. D. Giddens/G**	**2006–2008**	**Boston Celtics**	**1st/30th**
2010	Darlington Hobson/G	2009–2010	Milwaukee Bucks	2nd/37th
2013	**Tony Snell/G**	**2010–2013**	**Chicago Bulls**	**1st/20th**
2014	Cameron Bairstow/F	2010–2014	Chicago Bulls	2nd/49th

SEASON	AVERAGE ATTENDANCE	NATIONAL RANK	RECORD
1966–1967	12,778	2nd	14–1
1967–1968	11,920	5th	16–2
1968–1969	13,665	3rd	12–2
1969–1970	13,673	3rd	10–4
1970–1971	14,144	2nd	10–5
1971–1972	13,333	6th	12–2
1972–1973	14,352	6th	13–1
1973–1974	14,528	4th	15–0
1974–1975	14,025	4th	11–4
1975–1976	15,439	2nd	12–4
1976–1977	15,770	2nd	15–3
1977–1978	17,235	2nd	16–1
1978–1979	16,291	3rd	15–2
1979–1980	14,838	7th	6–12
1980–1981	17,033	3rd	9–7
1981–1982	16,525	4th	13–3
1982–1983	16,334	4th	13–4
1983–1984	15,701	7th	16–4
1984–1985	16,248	4th	14–6
1985–1986	17,050	4th	14–4
1986–1987	15,695	8th	19–4
1987–1988	15,875	9th	19–2
1988–1989	17,201	8th	15–5
1989–1990	16,629	8th	17–3
1990–1991	17,355	7th	15–2
1991–1992	15,605	11th	15–5
1992–1993	16,144	7th	15–1
1993–1994	16,648	8th	16–1
1994–1995	16,085	9th	12–8
1995–1996	16,026	9th	19–1
1996–1997	17,173	6th	18–0
1997–1998	17,625	7th	15–1
1998–1999	17,386	6th	19–1
1999–2000	16,443	8th	13–7
2000–2001	16,418	8th	15–4
2001–2002	16,426	7th	14–5
2002–2003	15,186	12th	10–7

Attendance at the Pit by Year (*continued*)

SEASON	AVERAGE ATTENDANCE	NATIONAL RANK	RECORD
2003–2004	14,679	15th	14–4
2004–2005	14,309	14th	18–1
2005–2006	13,387	21st	15–2
2006–2007	12,853	23rd	13–5
2007–2008	14,361	18th	16–2
2008–2009	13,994	17th	16–2
2009–2010*	13,595	22nd	17–1
2010–2011	14,570	16th	14–3
2011–2012	14,455	16th	14–2
2012–2013	15,022	16th	15–1
2013–2014	15,212	16th	13–2
2014–2015	14,571	18th	10–5
2015–2016	13,031	24th	12–4

* Pit renovations dropped official capacity to 15,411

The Pit's Top 10 Crowds (Men's Games)

ATTENDANCE	DATE	OPPONENT	SCORE
19,452	January 17, 1976	UNLV	UNLV 80–73
18,796	February 9, 1978	Arizona	UNM 103–85
18,676	January 24, 1976	Arizona	Arizona 80–79
18,670	February 11, 1978	Arizona	UNM 103–93
18,614	Januar 17, 1978	UNLV	UNM 89–76
18,490	December 9, 1975	NMSU	UNM 85–70
18,372	January 28, 1984	UTEP	UTEP 60–59
18,309	December 20, 1986	NMSU	UNM 64–50
18,192	January 25, 1986	UTEP	UTEP 71–70 OT
18,188	January 23, 1976	Arizona	UNM 65–63

The Pit's Top 10 Crowds (Women's Games)

ATTENDANCE	DATE	OPPONENT	SCORE
18,018	February 23, 1999	UTEP	UNM 64–61
18,018	February 5, 2000	BYU	UNM 65–59
18,018	March 28, 2001	Ohio State	Ohio State 64–61
18,018	February 1, 2003	UNLV	UNM 65–60
18,018	January 31, 2004	UNLV	UNM 70–66
17,578	March 8, 2003	BYU	UNM 63–44
17,472	March 6, 2004	CSU	CSU 59–52
17,215	January 6, 2002	UNLV	UNLV 62–53
17,213	February 4, 1997	Utah	Utah 53–49 (OT)
17,166	February 26, 2000	CSU	UNM 67–59

More than just the home for Lobo basketball, the Pit also played host to (in order):

1968	Olympic trials
1968	NCAA West Regional
1978	NCAA West Regional
1983	NCAA Final Four
1985	NCAA West Regional, first and second rounds
1988	McDonald's High School All-American Game
1992	NCAA West Regional
1996	NCAA West Regional, first and second rounds
2000	NCAA West Regional
2002	NCAA West Regional, first and second rounds
2003	NCAA Women's, first and second rounds
2003	NCAA Women's Midwest Regionals
2004	NCAA Women's, first and second rounds
2005	NCAA Albuquerque Regional
2008	NCAA Women's, first and second rounds
2011	NCAA Women's, first and second rounds
2012	NCAA Men's, second and third rounds

The Pit also was a venue for women's NCAA Tournament action.

In 2003 UNM hosted the NCAA Women's Basketball Tournament for the first time, taking the first and second rounds along with the Midwest Regional. The "new tradition" continued in 2004, with the first and second rounds contested in the Duke City. In 2006 the NCAA used the Pit for a regional. In 2008 and 2009 the NCAA placed the first and second rounds in the Pit again. And after the $60 million renovation, the Pit hosted NCAA first and second rounds in 2011.

Top 30 Collegiate Scorers in the Pit (Lobos except where noted)

POINTS	GAME	DATE
50	Marvin Johnson vs. CSU	March 2, 1978
47	Kenny Page vs. Illinois Tech	December 21, 1979
46	Marvin Johnson vs. Kentucky State	December 5, 1977
44	Kenny Page vs. UTEP	March 1, 1980
44	Kenny Page vs. BYU	January 15, 1981
43	Ruben Douglas vs. Wyoming	February 15, 2003
42	Bruce King (Iowa) vs. Pitt	December 30, 1976
42	Greg Brown vs. UTEP	February 5, 1994
41	Ben Monroe vs. BYU	February 23, 1967
41	Timo Saarelainen (BYU) vs. UNM	February 7, 1985
40	Ruben Douglas vs. UNLV	January 27, 2003
39	Lamont Long vs. Alcorn State	November 27, 1999
39	Donta Richardson (Wyoming) vs. UNM	February 15, 2003
39	Ruben Douglas vs. Utah	March 1, 2003
38	Kenny Page vs. Air Force	February 28, 1981
38	Bill Warner (Arizona) vs. UNM	January 17, 1970
38	Kenny Page vs. CSU	February 7, 1980
38	Brett Crawford (US International) vs. UNM	January 3, 1984
38	Ron Simpson (Rider) vs. UNM	December 23, 1987
38	Brett Merriweather (Texas Pan-Am) vs. UNM	December 8, 1998
37	Charles Smith vs. Hawaii	February 22, 1997
37	Bobby Phills (Southern) vs. Manhattan	December 28, 1990
37	Pete Cross (San Francisco) vs. UNM	December 20, 1968
36	Greg Howard vs. Arizona	February 8, 1969
36	Willie Long vs. St. Joseph's	December 19, 1969
36	Johnny Brown vs. Alaska-Anchorage	December 28, 1984
36	Johnny Brown vs. San Diego State	March 1, 1986
36	David Evans (CSU) vs. BYU	March 7, 1996
36	Ruben Douglas vs. Southern Utah	December 21, 2002
36	J. R. Giddens vs. Wyoming	February 9, 2008

The Rio Grande Rivalry

The rivalry between the University of New Mexico and New Mexico State University is one that is matched by few and that dates back to the early days.

The first competition began with football on January 1, 1894—the Lobos' first competition against another four-year institution.

The first basketball game was played on December 22, 1904, almost eight years before the territory of New Mexico became a state.

The Rio Grande Rivalry encompasses sports for both programs and is officially recognized as starting in the 2007–2008 academic year. Head-to-head competition in every sport is used to determing the winner on an annual basis. The series is not only for the current student-athletes competing in the sports but also to build school spirit and pride in the alumni and in fans of New Mexico who cheer for the Lobos or the Aggies.

Through the end of the 2015–2016 season, UNM has won the Rio Grande Rivalry for all eight years the trophy has been available. The rivalry series is a points-based system and is awarded to the school with the most points in all competitions. The specific scoring system is listed below for individual and team sports.

The winner of the rivalry series receives a trophy bearing the inscription of the annual winners and retains possession of it until the award presentation the following year.

The following lists the scores of the men's and women's UNM-NMSU games played in the Pit.

UNM Men vs. New Mexico State

DATE	WINNING TEAM	SCORE
February 9, 1967	UNM	65–57
February 7, 1968	UNM	72–71
March 16, 1968	NMSU	62–58
February 1, 1969	UNM	68–66
December 8, 1969	NMSU	90–83
December 22, 1970	UNM	72–66
December 4, 1971	UNM	78–76
December 5, 1972	UNM	88–67
December 11, 1973	UNM	72–71
December 3, 1974	UNM	69–58
December 9, 1975	UNM	85–70
December 22, 1976	NMSU	75–71
December 21, 1977	UNM	106–78
December 9, 1978	UNM	81–74
December 12, 1979	NMSU	103–84
November 29, 1980	UNM	97–79
December 12, 1981	NMSU	85–81
December 23, 1982	UNM	78–74 (double overtime)
December 22, 1983	UNM	57–51

UNM Men vs. New Mexico State *(continued)*

DATE	WINNING TEAM	SCORE
December 4, 1984	NMSU	67–64
December 23, 1985	UNM	54–44
December 20, 1986	UNM	64–50
December 3, 1987	UNM	72–71
December 17, 1988	UNM	64–61
December 7, 1989	NMSU	74–73
December 7, 1990	NMSU	80–73
December 23, 1992	UNM	71–66
December 11, 1993	NMSU	112–104 (double overtime)
December 17, 1994	NMSU	96–89
December 8, 1995	UNM	91–75
December 13, 1996	UNM	84–82 (overtime)
November 19, 1997	UNM	80–79
January 2, 1999	UNM	77–66
December 23, 1999	NMSU	63–60
January 6, 2001	NMSU	79–68 (overtime)
December 16, 2001	UNM	70–49
December 15, 2002	NMSU	72–60
December 22, 2003	UNM	64–49
December 1, 2004	UNM	99–80
December 13, 2005	UNM	71–68 (overtime)
November 28, 2006	UNM	79–76
December 19, 2007	UNM	83–69
December 23, 2008	UNM	76–62
December 5, 2009	UNM	75–58
December 11, 2010	UNM	78–62
November 16, 2011	NMSU	62–53
December 15, 2012	UNM	73–58
December 17, 2013	NMSU	67–61
December 3, 2014	UNM	62–47
December 16. 2015	UNM	79–61

UNM Women vs. NMSU

DATE	WINNING TEAM	SCORE
February 28, 1976	UNM	74–65
January 6, 1978	UNM	63–54
March 3, 1978	UNM	77–69
January 20, 1979	UNM	103–71
February 11, 1980	UNM	76–62
March 5, 1980	NMSU	73–71
February 16, 1981	NMSU	79–65
November 23, 1981	NMSU	60–59
February 5, 1983	UNM	81–73
February 18, 1984	UNM	57–41
February 23, 1985	NMSU	65–56
January 25, 1986	NMSU	66–49
March 3, 1987	NMSU	78–74
January 13, 1992	NMSU	83–57
December 30, 1992	NMSU	63–49
November 27, 1993	NMSU	70–55
December 17, 1994	NMSU	73–58
December 22, 1995	NMSU	78–73 (triple overtime)
December 21, 1996	UNM	63–44
November 26, 1997	UNM	81–50
December 12, 1998	UNM	55–54
January 6, 2000	UNM	71–47
November 28, 2000	UNM	82–53
December 18, 2001	UNM	82–55
December 3, 2002	UNM	86–75
December 14, 2003	UNM	62–39
December 21, 2004	UNM	56–27
January 1, 2006	UNM	55–42
December 2, 2006	UNM	81–47
December 21, 2007	UNM	62–56
December 4, 2008	UNM	80–48
December 20, 2009	UNM	81–64
December 30, 2010	UNM	65–60
December 4, 2011	UNM	54–53
November 20, 2012	UNM	60–37
December 7, 2013	UNM	65–55
December 20, 2015	NMSU	52–47

Lobo Women's Top Marks

Top-10 scoring leaders (names in bold played for
Don Flanagan):

Dionne Marsh (2004–2008): 1,913 points
Abby Garchek (1994–1998): 1,836 points
Jordan Adams (1999–2003): 1,798 points
Alison Foote (1981–1985): 1,672 points
Jean Rostermundt (1977–1980): 1,541 points
Amy Beggin (2006–2010): 1,428 points
Yvonne McKinnon (1981–1985): 1,416 points
Miranda Sanchez (1998–2001): 1,301 points
Khadijah Shumpert (2013–2016): 1,192 points
Sonya Bryant (1996–2000): 1,142 points

Players with 1,000 points and 500 rebounds (names
in bold played for Don Flanagan):

Jean Rostermundt (1977–1980): 1,541 points,
607 rebounds
Alison Foote (1982–1985): 1,672 points,
800 rebounds
Yvonne McKinnon (1982–1985): 1,420 points,
857 rebounds
Tracy Satran (1984–1987): 1,027 points,
594 rebounds
Heidi Harris (1992–1995): 1,046 points,
669 rebounds
Tamika Stukes (1995–1998): 1,017 points,
606 rebounds
Miranda Sanchez (1998–2001): 1,301 points,
556 rebounds
Jordan Adams (2000–2003): 1,798 points,
729 rebounds
Lindsey Arndt (2002–2005): 1,073 points,
701 points
Mandi Moore (2002–2005): 1,057 points,
603 rebounds

Dionne Marsh (2005–2008): 1,913 points,
738 rebounds
Khadijah Shumpert (2013–2016): 1,192 points,
603 rebounds
Sara Halasz (2008–2014): 1,061 points, 557
rebounds

Fifty Years and Fifty Pit Stars

Ten Pit Stars from 1966 to 1980

Mel Daniels (1964–1967): Many UNM basketball
fans regard Daniels as the consummate Lobo
hoopster, capable of doing it all, after being
recruited to UNM by Bob King from Burlington
(Iowa) Junior College. Daniels capped his senior
season as a member of the first Lobo team to play
in the Pit when he led the WAC in scoring (21.5
points per game) and was an All-American. He led
the Lobos in scoring and rebounding in all three
seasons he played here. He went on to become
one of the ABA's all-time greatest players.

Ben Monroe (1964–1967): Like Mel Daniels, Monroe
only got to enjoy one season in the Lobos' new
arena, averaging 14.5 points per game and 8.8
rebounds per game, with 7.9 rebounds per game his
average when his Lobo years ended. He came out of
Carlsbad High School and is ranked among the top
10 in-state athletes to ever play for UNM, averaging
12.3 points per game and 8.1 rebounds per game
in his three seasons, two of which ended with NIT
appearances.

Ron Nelson (1966–1968): A native of Artesia, New
Mexico, Nelson came to UNM in 1966 after two years
at the New Mexico Military Institute in Roswell. He
played for Bob King for two seasons. In his senior
season of 1967–1968, UNM started 17–0, won the
WAC title, and advanced to the NCAA Tournament

for the first time. Nelson led the Lobos in scoring at 19.5 points per game while shooting 82.2 percent from the free-throw line.

Greg Howard (1967–1969): "Stretch" averaged 14.4 and then 19.7 points per game in his two seasons as a Lobo. He was a first-round pick (10th overall) by Phoenix in the 1970 NBA draft, and he played two seasons with the Suns, seeing action in 92 games over those two years. UNM didn't have many big men more mobile than 6′ 9″ "Stretch," basically a small forward packed into a big man's frame, and the guy who backed up Mel Daniels.

Petie Gibson (1968–1971): The 1968–1969 season began with high expectations, and the Lobos ranked in the top 10, but they dropped out after a string of road losses. Howard led a young team, scoring 19.7 points per game, with sophomores Willie Long and Gibson beginning their runs as three-year starters. He led UNM and the WAC in assists for three straight years and had 14 or more assists five times in his UNM career.

Willie Long (1968–1971): Coming to UNM as a center, Long averaged in double figures all three seasons, with 11.6 points per game as a sophomore and then back-to-back seasons of 23.9 points per game. He led the WAC in scoring as a senior and was All-WAC as a junior and again as a senior. He scored 41 points in a game against BYU in his junior season, and he hauled down 21 rebounds in a game as a sophomore. In the 1969–1970 season, he had eight double-doubles in a row.

Darryl Minniefield (1971–1973): An All-WAC first-teamer as a senior, Minniefield led the team in averaging 29.4 minutes on the floor per game, but his aggressiveness in the paint led to

15 disqualifications in his three seasons. (UNM career leader Daniel Faris fouled out 18 times in four seasons.) He averaged 11.0 points per game as a junior and then achieved a team-high 13.1 points per game as a senior, when he moved from a forward position to center for coach Norm Ellenberger.

Michael Cooper (1976–1978): One of the best all-around Lobos, Cooper could score and play defense at a high level. He went on to NBA fame with the Los Angeles Lakers, where he was a top NBA defender (just ask Larry Bird). In 1977–1978, the Cooper-paced Lobos led the nation in scoring, averaging more than 97 points per game. Cooper earned All-America honors after averaging 16.1 points per game, he was a third-round draft pick of the Los Angeles Lakers in 1978, and he spent his entire 12-year career in L.A., a member of five world championship teams in Los Angeles.

Marvin Johnson (1976–1978): Nobody but Cool Hand Luke can eat 50 eggs, and only Marvin Johnson (so far) can score 50 points in the Pit. Johnson hit 21 field goals and 8 free throws against Colorado State on March 2, 1978—before the 3-point line became part of the game. He led the Lobos in scoring in both of his seasons and was a second-round pick of the Chicago Bulls in the 1978 NBA draft.

Kenny Page (1979–1981): Page might have been the best-ever Lobo at using the backboard. Using his sweet touch, the southpaw led the Lobos in scoring during the "Lobogate" season, averaging 28 points per game. A transfer from Ohio State, he notched a career-high 47 points against Illinois State and 44 (his best in a WAC game) against both BYU and UTEP.

Phil Smith (1980–1984): Some Lobo fans will argue that Smith was UNM's best-ever point guard. He played with an ornery edge, was wet-leather tough, and could penetrate any defense. He missed 13 games with a broken foot as a junior, and thus he could have scored more than the 1,477 points he finished his career with. He was an All-WAC first-team selection as a senior—the fourth year in a row he led the Lobos in assists—and a fourth-round NBA draft pick in 1984.

Tim Garrett (1982–1984): Nicknamed "14 carat," Garrett earned letters both seasons and led UNM in scoring as a senior at 15.4 points per game. In 1984 he was a seventh-round pick of the Washington Bullets in the NBA draft.

George Scott (1982–1985): A two-year starter at Southern Idaho, Scott transferred to UNM and played one season (1982–1983) before sitting out 1983–1984 with a herniated disk in his back, which did not require surgery. After his senior season (1984–1985) he left UNM as its most-accurate shooter ever, sinking 62.2 percent of his shots in all games and 58.9 percent in WAC games. He averaged 14 points per game in his two seasons as a Lobo.

Hunter Greene (1983–1988): Upon graduation, Greene was UNM's all-time leading scorer. He still ranks in the top 10 in career scoring at UNM and holds the distinction of being the only Lobo with 1,500 points, 600 rebounds, 300 assists, and 200 steals, with the program record for most steals in a season (84 in 1986–1987). He serves as an analyst on games aired on KKOB-AM.

Kelvin Scarborough (1983–1987): Is this the quickest Lobo ever? Scarborough was a jet on the court and left UNM number one in steals while also entering the 1,000-Point Club. He once had 21 assists in a game. He averaged 18.6 points per game as a senior, including a team-high 34 in an 84–68 victory over Brown in the first round of the Creamland Lobo Invitational on December 26, 1986.

Johnny Brown (1984–1986): A transfer from Loyola-Marymount, Brown left UNM after his two seasons as the school's seventh-leading scorer all-time with 1,157 points. He scored 649 points in the 1985–1986 season, then he had the third-best total for a single season and scored on 56.9 percent of his shots as a Lobo. He was an All-WAC selection as a senior, when he led UNM in scoring and rebounding, and an honorable-mention All-American by the Associated Press.

Luc Longley (1987–1991): When this Australian departed, he was UNM's all-time leading scorer, rebounder, and shot-blocker, and he became the seventh player taken in the NBA draft, by the Minnesota Timberwolves. He later played with the NBA champion Chicago Bulls. In 2016 he was inducted into the New Mexico Sports Hall of Fame.

Rob Robbins (1987–1991): This former Farmington High standout, who was also quite a baseball player, was one of the most-popular Lobos and still owns the mark for consecutive free throws, making 52 in a row in 1989–1990. When he left UNM he was the third-leading scorer, he held all of UNM's 3-point records, and he was the ninth-most-accurate free-throw shooter (88.8 percent; 309 of 348) in NCAA history.

Charlie Thomas (1987–1989): Not many two-year Lobo players managed to score more than 1,000 points and grab 500 rebounds, but Thomas did it, after transferring to UNM from Wake Forest. In both of his Lobo seasons, he led the team in scoring and rebounding, and he was the WAC Newcomer of the Year in 1987–1988. Twice he hauled down 16 rebounds.

Willie Banks (1988-1992): This former Albuquerque High standout didn't take long to show he could play at the next level, scoring a career-high 28 points in a game against George Washington University in his freshman season. After his freshman year, he was second in the balloting for WAC Newcomer of the Year. Banks finished his four-year career at UNM with 1,394 points.

Ten Pit Stars from 1991 to 2000

Greg Brown (1992–1994): Brown demonstrated that a 5' 7" guard can get the job done! He did so by taking the UNM Lobos all the way to the 1994 WAC basketball championship; without Brown—who played two seasons at New Mexico Junior College— the Lobos wouldn't have come close to winning that WAC title, the school's first in over 16 years. He was named the winner of the Frances Pomeroy Naismith Award, given annually to the best player in the nation under six feet.

Charles Smith (1993–1997): Finishing his UNM career with 1,993 points, "Spider" became the school's scoring leader in a February 3, 1997, game versus BYU. His nearly 2,000 points were the 11th-best total in WAC history, and he helped UNM get to three NCAA tournaments during his stint at UNM. He was one of three Lobos—along with Francis Grant and Mel Daniels—to lead UNM in scoring for three years in a row. The Miami Heat selected Smith in the first round of the 1997 NBA draft.

David Gibson (1994–1998): This point guard played locally at Sandia High, and he became a four-year starter at that position for the Lobos. He started in 125 of the 128 UNM games he played in, and although he wasn't looked at to supply a lot of points, he played exceptional defense and was a vocal team leader.

Royce Olney (1994–1998): Once a prep great for Hot Springs High School, and the Class AA Player of the Year as a senior, some fans wondered what Head Coach Dave Bliss was thinking when he recruited Olney to UNM. Four years later, he was regarded as one of the grittiest, most determined players to wear the Lobos uniform. His career ended prematurely when he suffered an ACL injury 25 games into his senior season—and the Lobos were 3–4 without him.

Clayton Shields (1994–1998): Shields cracked the starting lineup as a freshman and responded with 10.5 points per game and 4.8 rebounds per game to make the WAC all-newcomer team. He finished his career with 1,837 points (14.4 per game) and 758 rebounds and was co-WAC player of the year.

Kenny Thomas (1995–1999): Only one Lobo has scored more points than Kenny Thomas's 1,931 points: Charles Smith. Thomas was arguably one of the most popular players in UNM history, after playing at nearby Albuquerque High. Twice he scored 31 points, and another time he grabbed 18 rebounds in a game. UNM enjoyed its best four-season mark in school history with Thomas on the roster. He was a first-round draft pick by the Philadelphia 76ers in 1999.

Lamont Long (1996–2000): This four-year Lobo starter became the 11th member of the 1,000-point, 500-rebound club during his junior season, after which he made himself eligible for the NBA draft, then changed his mind and returned to the fold. He led the MWC in scoring as a senior, when he was a first-team All-MWC pick. He scored 50 points in an exhibition game against the California All-Stars as his junior season began, and he poured in 39 points against Alcorn State in his senior season.

Kevin Henry (1997–2000): After playing in all 32 games as a freshman in 1997–1998, this guard was named to the WAC All-Newcomer team. He started 33 of the team's 34 games the next season and averaged 12.8 points per game while establishing a UNM record for 3-pointers, with 102. He started all 32 games as a junior and scored in the double-digits 13 times, including 18 points in UNM's upset win at Arizona. He sat out the 2000–2001 season after transferring to Baylor to compete his career.

Marlon Parmer (1999–2001): Parmer was coach Fran Fraschilla's first recruit, but things didn't work out well for this guard, who averaged 11.6 points per game and 4 rebounds per game in his first season at UNM. After starting 13 of UNM's first 16 games in 2000–2001, averaging 12.8 points per game and 5.4 assists per contest, Fraschilla's "abrasive style" had Parmer packing—the ninth Lobo to depart—and ultimately heading to Kentucky Wesleyan.

Wayland White (1999–2001): White was touted as one of UNM's most flamboyant dunkers and shot-blockers, and for good reason. White, who transferred to UNM after two years at Iowa Western Community College, was the first Lobo to record 100 steals and 100 blocks in a career, and in 2000–2001 he was the only player in the nation to lead his conference in steals and blocks.

Ten Pit Stars from 2001 to 2010

Ruben Douglas (2000–2003): "Credited" with rewriting the school and MWC record books in his senior season, this transfer from the University of Arizona led the nation in scoring—the first Lobo

to do so—in the 2002–2003 season, averaging 27.96 points per game. He ended his three-year stint at UNM with 1,782 points, good for fifth place on the all-time scoring list at UNM. He was one of two Lobos (with Danny Granger) named to the MWC's 10th Anniversary Team in October 2008.

David Chiotti (2002–2006): Chiotti became the ninth player in UNM history with 1,100 points and 600 rebounds, and he was known as a player who improved every year during his career. He was a third-team All-MWC pick as a junior and a second-teamer as a senior. In his final three seasons, he led UNM in field-goal percentage and wound up his career making a ninth-best (at UNM) 53.7 percent of his shots, en route to 1,145 points.

Mark Walters (2002–2006): A local product—from Highland High School—Walters finished his freshman season with 265 points, the ninth-best total by a Lobo frosh. He was a first-team All-WAC performer as a senior. Showing his versatility, he finished second in MWC history with 153 career steals, and he fell just 17 rebounds short of becoming the 14th Lobo with 1,000 points and 500 rebounds in his career.

Danny Granger (2003–2005): After transferring from Bradley, Granger became eligible in January 2004 and began contributing right away, starting the 22 games that remained that season and all 30 in the next. He averaged 18.9 points per game and 8.9 rebounds per game as a junior, and then 16.7 points per game and 8.2 rebounds per game as a senior, when he became the first player in school history to get 60 assists, 60 blocks, and 60 steals in a season. He won the MWC Tournament MVP award and led the Lobos to the 2005 NCAA tournament. He was a first-round draft pick of Indianapolis, and the 17th player taken, in 2005. He played with the Pacers in 2005–2013, then was with the L.A. Clippers in 2013–2014 and the Phoenix Suns in 2014–2015. He was one of two Lobos (with Ruben Douglas) named to the MWC's 10th Anniversary Team in October 2008.

Tony Danridge (2004–2009): Maybe best known for his highlight-reel slam dunks, Danridge rebounded from a broken left leg after his junior season to claim first-team All-MWC honors in 2009. In his senior season, he averaged a team-high 1.9 points per game, with seven games of 20-plus points. He finished his UNM career with 1,260 points.

Chad Toppert (2005–2009): In his four years at UNM, this son of a former Lobo managed to eclipse the 1,000-point scoring barrier with just 28 career starts. An excellent 3-point shooter, he was ranked in the nation's top 10 in 3-point percentage in 2007 and 2008, earning All-MWC honorable mention both times. He ranks second all-time at UNM in career 3-pointers with 266, hitting 43.9 percent of his attempts from behind the arc.

J. R. Giddens (2006–2008): Unhappy after two years at Kansas, Giddens transferred to UNM and, after sitting out the 2005–2006 season, he averaged 15.8 points per game as a junior and then led the MWC in field goals (with 210) as the conference's Player of the Year in 2007–2008. He was a first-round draft pick, the 30th player overall, taken by the Boston Celtics in 2008. He played sparingly for the Celtics for two seasons, and he saw action in 11 games with the N.Y. Knicks in 2009–2010.

Roman Martinez (2006–2010): This likeable El Paso native was the first Lobo to reach 1,000 points, 600 rebounds, 200 3-pointers, and 200 assists in a career, which ended with his selection as the recipient of the Chip Hilton Award, given for outstanding character, leadership, and talent. Also as a senior he was named an Academic All-American, UNM"s first such honoree in 35 years. March 3, 2010, was proclaimed "Roman Martinez Day" in New Mexico by Governor Bill Richardson.

Dairese Gary (2007–2011): A two-time All-MWC selection and a two-time All-MWC defensive player, Gary owned the MWC records for career assists and assists in MWC games heading into the 2015–2016 season, and he concluded his sparkling career at UNM with the satisfaction of having seen his team win at least 22 games in all four of his seasons, with 98 victories in all. He was often asked to guard the opponent's top scoring threat.

Phillip McDonald (2008–2012): McDonald's stint at UNM saw his teams win a total of 102 games, the most wins for a scholarship player, and those teams combined for three MWC regular-season championships and played in four postseason tournaments. He is tied for fifth all-time in 3-pointers, and he canned a career-high seven treys as a sophomore in a game at Air Force. He started 100 of the 133 games he played in while at UNM, finishing with 1,146 points.

Ten Pit Stars from 2011 to 2016

Cameron Bairstow (2010–2014): This Aussie is one of the most highly decorated Lobos in program history, scoring 1,239 points in his four-year career and named a second-team All-American by *Sports Illustrated* after one of the greatest senior seasons in the school's history, capped by being named MVP of the MWC Tournament. He became the first Lobo to average points per game in the double digits (with 20.4) after averaging single figures, which he did three years in a row for his first three seasons (2.6, 3.7, and 9.7 points per game in 2010–2011, 2011–2012, and 2012–2013, respectively). He was a member of the Australia national team in the 2016 Summer Olympic Games in Rio de Janeiro, Brazil.

Drew Gordon (2010–2012): After just over a season at UCLA, Gordon opted to head to UNM instead of taking the offer of other suitors, including San Diego State and UNLV of the MWC and Notre Dame. He started the last 19 games of the 2010–2011 season after sitting out 2009–2010. He averaged 13 points per game and 10.5 rebounds per game, leading the Lobos in rebounding for 21 games, and he scored in double digits 22 times. Gordon was named the conference's Newcomer of the Year in 2011, also earning All-MWC second-team laurels. He played in nine games with the Philadelphia 76ers in 2014–2015, then he headed to the D-League for some seasoning.

Alex Kirk (2010–2014): A Los Alamos native and a former star with the Hilltoppers there, Kirk broke the 1,000-point barrier in the MWC championship game in his senior season, becoming only the eighth New Mexican to accomplish that at UNM. A two-time All-MWC player and All-MWC defensive selection, he holds the freshman record at UNM for points in a game with 31 against Cal State-Bakersfield.

Tony Snell (2010–2013): Lobo fans think Snell took a gamble when he opted for the NBA draft over a senior season in 2013, after he averaged 12.5 points per game for the team in 2012–2013 and was a vital cog in the Lobos' climb to the conference's regular-season and tournament titles. The conference tournament MVP, his gamble paid off when the Chicago Bulls drafted him as their 20th pick in the first round, and he became the eighth first-round draft choice in Lobo history and the sixth since 1991. Snell said at the time he planned to complete his degree as a UNM graduate.

Kendall Williams (2010–2014): Williams was the fourth player in UNM history to be voted All-MWC first team in back-to-back seasons after finishing seventh in the league in scoring, fifth in 3-point percentage, second in steals, second in assists, and second in assist-to-turnover ratio; he also made the All-Defensive team. Averaging 16.4 points per game as a senior, he was the only player in the MWC with three games of nine or more assists and one or fewer turnovers.

Hugh Greenwood (2011–2015): One the most-popular Lobos, this Australian became just the second guard in school history with more than 1,000 points and 600 rebounds (Lamont Long was the first). Among UNM's top 10 all-time in career minutes played, assists, and 3-pointers, he was a key part of Lobo teams that won five conference championships.

Deshawn Delaney (2013–2015): After two seasons at Vincennes, Delaney was voted an honorable-mention selection on the all-conference team, having improved his scoring, rebounding, assists, steals, and blocks from his junior season after becoming an everyday starter in his senior season. Sadly, he broke a bone in his right hand two days before the Senior Night game. He was given an honorary start against Wyoming on March 7, 2015, then he was subbed three seconds into the game after the Cowboys conceded the opening tip. He exited the game to a standing ovation and shared an emotional, memorable embrace with Head Coach Craig Neal.

Cullen Neal (2013–2016): The son of coach Craig Neal, this slick-shooting 6′ 5″ guard came out of Eldorado High School and became an enigma for Lobos fans. Half the fans seemed to love him, and the other half thought of him as a "Daddy's boy" and ultimately caused him to leave UNM for Ole Miss after a disappointing 2015–2016 season. A May 2016 graduate of UNM, Neal still had two years of eligibility left for the Rebels. Neal averaged 12.3 points per game and 3.7 assists per game in 2015–2016, while shooting 35 percent from the field and committing 101 turnovers.

Elijah Brown (2015–Present): Brown was the Lobos' fourth Newcomer of the Year honoree after he led UNM in scoring in his first season with 21.7 points per game, when he was one of the nation's leading free-throw shooters. He also was named to the All-MWC first team. The son of veteran NBA coach Mike Brown, his college career began at Butler University.

Tim Williams (2015–Present): The Lobos' leading rebounder and most efficient shooter, Williams led the MWC in shooting (60.4 percent), becoming the third Lobo ever to shoot 60 percent or better with over 300 attempts (215 of 356) in a season. He averaged 16.8 points per game and a team-best 7.4 boards in his first season with UNM, which concluded with being named to the All-MWC second team.